More praise for *Finding the Sweet Spot*

"The successful innovators I know constantly struggle to balance the passion they need to push ahead and the dispassion essential to integrity. *Finding the Sweet Spot* does a superb job of packaging, prioritizing and explaining how to achieve the balance that empowers sustainable innovation."
—MICHAEL SCHRAGE, MIT Researcher and author of *Serious Play*

"Everything I know about life, work, the environment, and entrepreneurship tells me that Dave Pollard is right. Do yourself and the world a favor and read this book."
—THOMAS H. DAVENPORT, President's Distinguished Professor of Information Technology and Management, Babson College

"No advice can change the world, if you leave it on the shelf. But if you read this you can see the crucial threads Dave Pollard has woven together. And then maybe you can change the world. Go do that."
—BILL TOZIER, Vague Innovation, LLC, and co-founder of NotAnEmployee.org

"It has long been said: to make change, begin with yourself. Dave Pollard's approach will make many who want change but feel worn down by their lives find a path to reconnect with their values—and begin anew, by finding their own 'sweet spot' of passion for their work, and the places and people that will fill their lives."
—BRUCE A. STEWART, futurist, philosopher, writer, and CEO of Accendor Research.

"Have you been waiting for the moment to just frigging do something about having a satisfying work life? Then pick up this book! Don't let your fears or objections stop you. Follow the path Dave lays out and you will not only make your life better, you'll make the world a better place through the reflected joy of your own fulfillment and by meeting real needs with new business ideas. Do it!"
—NANCY WHITE, founder of Full Circle Associates

"I can't believe this essential book has never been written before! Thanks to Dave Pollard, it's here now, and now that it is let's make it required reading for all those young people (and many others, like those about to embark on career number two, three, or four) who need a hand charting a course to the future they are about to invent."
—JOHN ABRAMS, founder and CEO of South Mountain Company and author of *Companies We Keep: Employee Ownership and the Business of Community and Place*

"Dave Pollard explains why finding your right work is a good thing for you and for our society and our planet. He offers unique perspectives on work, enterprise and social responsibility that resonate as true. This is an important book. Read it for yourself, and also for the rest of us."
—DICK RICHARDS, author of *Artful Work* and *Is Your Genius At Work?*

"*Finding the Sweet Spot* provides a holistic framework for entrepreneurship. It can help you discover your own power, find the right partners, and experiment at the margin of what you know and the human needs you can fulfill. If you consider yourself an entrepreneur, or want to unleash your creative side, or want to be an agent of positive change, or if now is the time for broader perspective—share this book."
> —Ross Mayfield, Chairman, President, and Cofounder of Socialtext

"Dave Pollard is an undaunted observer of our world. He navigates its challenges and promises with passion and curiosity and an eye to designing a path of personal and social sustainability. No 21st century citizen should travel without this map!"
> —Chris Corrigan, Principal at Harvest Moon Consultants, Ltd.

"I love this book; it is beautifully written. I believe that in a few years time the majority of people and businesses will be working passionately and productively for the benefit of society and each other. *Finding the Sweet Spot* brings that day much closer with its practical and well informed approach. Anyone who reads this book will not spend another day feeling frustrated by the way they make their living. With the help of this book they will find a way to turn their passions into profit for themselves and for us all."
> —Neil Crofts, author of *Authentic Business*

"I finished *Finding the Sweet Spot* in one night, but I carried it around with me for two weeks after, for no other reason than I wanted people to ask me what I was reading. It worked. This book led to a series of blissfully rich conversations with friends and strangers alike, and something in my heart believes that it's because we all have in us a deep and heartfelt desire to ask and pursue the crucial questions it addresses."
> —Siona van Dijk, Director of Gaia.com

"Dave Pollard is a bridge between two worlds—the world of liberated imagination and the world of bottom line results. If you are serious about making innovation real in your life, read this book."
> —Mitch Ditkoff, author of *Awake at the Wheel: Getting Your Great Ideas Rolling (in an Uphill World)* and co-founder and President of Idea Champions

"In *Finding the Sweet Spot*, Dave gently but firmly guides the reader toward finding their true calling in life. I am going to ask everyone I love to read it. I'm particularly struck by the message that you can't go it alone, and by the fundamental importance of social ties, both strong and weak; how engagement with the wider community around you, through social networking and respect for all of your stakeholders, is key to the success of a Natural Enterprise."
> —Christian Crumlish, author of *The Power of Many: How the Living Web is Transforming Politics, Business, and Everyday Life*

FINDING THE SWEET SPOT

FINDING THE SWEET SPOT

the natural entrepreneur's guide to responsible, sustainable, joyful work

DAVE POLLARD

CHELSEA GREEN PUBLISHING COMPANY
White River Junction, Vermont

Our Commitment to Green Publishing

Chelsea Green sees publishing as a tool for cultural change and ecological stewardship. We strive to align our book manufacturing practices with our editorial mission and to reduce the impact of our business enterprise on the environment. We print our books and catalogs on chlorine-free recycled paper, using soy-based inks whenever possible. This book may cost slightly more because we use recycled paper, and we hope you'll agree that it's worth it. Chelsea Green is a member of the Green Press Initiative (www.greenpressinitiative.org), a nonprofit coalition of publishers, manufacturers, and authors working to protect the world's endangered forests and conserve natural resources.

Finding the Sweet Spot was printed on 55 lb Natures Book Natural, a 30-percent post-consumer-waste recycled, FSC-certified paper supplied by Thomson Shore.

Developmental Editor: Shay Totten
Project Manager: Emily Foote
Copy Editor: Susan Barnett
Proofreader: Ellen Brownstein
Indexer: Christy Stroud
Book Designer: Peter Holm

First printing, September 2008
10 9 8 7 6 5 4 3 2 1   08 09 10 11 12

Library of Congress Cataloging-in-Publication Data
Pollard, Dave, 1951–
   Finding the sweet spot: the natural entrepreneur's guide to responsible, sustainable, joyful work / Dave Pollard.
       p. cm.
   Includes bibliographical references and index.
   ISBN 978-1-933392-90-5
   1. Entrepreneurship. I. Title.

HB615.P64 2008
658.1'1--dc22
            2008017907

Chelsea Green Publishing Company
Post Office Box 428
White River Junction, VT 05001
(802) 295-6300
www.chelseagreen.com

The Chelsea Green Publishing Company is committed to preserving ancient forests and natural resources. We elected to print this title on 30% postconsumer recycled paper, processed chlorine-free. As a result, for this printing, we have saved:

17 Trees (40' tall and 6-8" diameter)
6,271 Gallons of Wastewater
12 million BTU's Total Energy
805 Pounds of Solid Waste
1,511 Pounds of Greenhouse Gases

Chelsea Green Publishing made this paper choice because we and our printer, Thomson-Shore, Inc., are members of the Green Press Initiative, a nonprofit program dedicated to supporting authors, publishers, and suppliers in their efforts to reduce their use of fiber obtained from endangered forests. For more information, visit: www.greenpressinitiative.org.

Environmental impact estimates were made using the Environmental Defense Paper Calculator. For more information visit: www.papercalculator.org.

CONTENTS

AN OPEN LETTER TO READERS

becoming a model natural enterprise for others to follow

In our modern society, we rely on the education system to teach us what we need to know to live and make a living.

That system has let us down badly. It is in the interest of those who control the current economic system, those with the established wealth and power, that we not know that there is a better way to make a living than working for them, doing meaningless work as wage slaves, just to buy ourselves some leisure time to do what has meaning for us.

We each need, personally, to rediscover the joy and meaning of natural work, of Natural Entrepreneurship. This book is an attempt to get you started on that journey.

> We need a blossoming of millions of Natural Enterprises, connected and collaborating and supporting each other as part of a dynamic Natural Economy.

But what we also need, collectively, as a society, is a blossoming of thousands, millions of Natural Enterprises, connected and collaborating and supporting each other generously as part of a dynamic new Natural Economy.

Is such a thing possible?

Buckminster Fuller, who accomplished some pretty amazing things in his areas of expertise, said:

> You never change things by fighting the existing reality. To change something, build a new model that makes the existing model obsolete.

And Margaret Mead, the famous anthropologist, chimed in:

> Never doubt that a small group of thoughtful, committed citizens can change the world. Indeed, it is the only thing that ever has.

This is where you come in.

I'm asking you to do more than just freeing yourself from a life of grinding, miserable, meaningless work by creating your own Natural Enterprise.

I'm asking you to join me in being a part of a model "that makes the existing model obsolete."

A model of a million Natural Enterprises, all communities within their own physical communities, the places they live and call home, and all communities within a new community of Natural Economy.

It's not enough that I show you, dear readers, the way to create a Natural Enterprise, and start you on this journey. We owe it to our larger community, our fragile planet struggling under the oppressive weight of an industrial economy that is destroying it, the larger community of all-life-on-Earth, that we take heart from Bucky Fuller and courage from Margaret Mead and create, together, a model that will show the world that there is a better way to make a living, and a better way to live.

We can do this. This Natural Economy could come about as quickly and miraculously as the Industrial Economy was ushered in by the steam engine and the division of labor, and could transform the way we make a living just as dramatically.

This Natural Economy is nothing more than a huge Natural Enterprise in which we will all be, *must* all be, partners. Its collective Purpose is nothing less than to save the world. Between us, we have the collective Gifts and collective Passions and the capacities and knowledge that are "on Purpose" to make it happen.

When you first go to the Natural Enterprise Web site you will find a Pledge. This Pledge is to join in equal partnership with others creating Natural Enterprises, to *be a model*, to *help show the whole world a better way to make a living*, responsibly, sustainably, joyfully.

Please join me in taking that Pledge, and becoming part of what might be, through the power of people, knowledge, innovation, partnership, collaboration, and generosity, the most important enterprise the world has ever known.

DAVE POLLARD

January, 2008

FOREWORD

During the seventies—when high unemployment and energy short-ages were a daily fact of life—some friends and I started and ran a very successful natural food cooperative in Menlo Park, California, called Briarpatch Natural Foods. It was created to fill a real community need, following the age-old busi-ness adage of "find a need and fill it." People had time on their hands, and natural foods were expensive, so by working eight hours every three months, members were able to purchase healthy foods for at least 30 percent less. Three of us co-managed the store, and the work of unloading trucks, stocking shelves, buying fresh produce at the produce terminal, running the cash registers, and everything else needed to operate a small grocery store was done by members. At one point, there were more than 350 families on the waiting list.

Because labor is, by far, the largest expense of doing business, taking most of that cost out of the expense statement created not only cheaper food but also an enormous forgiveness for the obvi-ous inefficiencies of volunteer, untrained labor and the lack of basic business skills by its enthusiastic and smart, but woefully unskilled management. Oh, but what fun we had playing store!

It eventually proved to be unsustainable in the long term for the simple fact that business is cyclical and when Silicon Valley exploded into runaway growth and success, no one had time to play store, and the store didn't adapt quickly enough to the rapidly changing times that did it in. All vendors were fully paid, all member invest-ments were fully returned, and the graceful ending left us only fond memories. By our current business standards, it was a failure because it didn't grow and make its "investors" a ton of money. For those of us most intimately involved in the daily business of running a community cooperative, it was one of our most beautiful, successful business experiences.

On the other hand, Smith & Hawken, the $100 million garden company I cofounded, is considered an enduring entrepreneurial success. I disagree, and here's why.

Smith & Hawken's original mission was to supply sturdy, well-made tools to very serious craftsmen (and women). We started with legendary garden tools made by a two-hundred-year-old company in England and sold them to small organic farmers and serious organic gardeners.

Because they were priced at four times the price of the poorly made, throwaway garden tools at the local hardware store, we thought there was a very limited market that would require us to work only part-time, leaving us room to do more important things. When we tried to branch out into woodworking tools, the customer base we had built the brand name on asked us what the hell we were doing. We told them we were a tool company and we wanted to sell other well-made tools. They let us know that we were not a tool company, we were an organic garden company, and they were uninterested in Japanese carpentry tools. All well and good, as our own personal values coincided with the altered company mission, and the company became a very successful garden company that listened to its customers and doubled in sales for many years, requiring typical entrepreneurial sacrifice and dedication.

But now, long after the founders have moved on to other pursuits, and the company has changed hands several times, it has been purchased by the largest home pesticide distributor in the United States, betraying the fundamental values of the brand, its founders, and many of its customers. A brand standing for good values will now be used as a halo around a company that stands in opposition to those values. For me, that's a failure.

You may say "big freaking deal, get on with your life" and that I have done. But values have always been what I wanted my life to be about, and what I consider anti-values are now associated with my name. A lesson learned.

Values are also what Dave Pollard and this book are ultimately about. As practical and groundbreaking as this book is, always lurking in the background is a question of values. Dave not only shows us how important it is to thoroughly research the real business opportunities that need filling, and teaches us how to do it, but also asks us to explore what it is we love doing and what we're good at as equally important to fulfill our yearnings to be useful and make the world a better place.

Yet this is not a warm and fuzzy "do-it-and-the-money-will-come" wish book. What you'll find here is an excellent, nonacademic, no-nonsense, down-to-earth, hands-on, "insight-full" working guidebook, led by an innovative, caring, and extremely bright man who may not know all the answers, but, much better, shows us how to go about finding them. However you may define business success and meaning for yourself, this will become one of those books you often turn to for idea sparks and troubleshooting; a manual that stays close by after you've dog-eared, starred, and underlined the pages most useful to you.

It is, most importantly, a timely book. I'm convinced that the coming changes will be a time that requires the most from each of us. As "big-corporate" and "big-government" failures to negotiate the transition to decentralized renewable energy and sustainable living become increasingly apparent, it will be up to each of us, especially those of us involved in small community business, to step up to the responsibility of meeting real local needs. Opportunities abound in cultural transitions, especially those that are potentially devastating if creative answers are not found and implemented.

It will be the combination of independent can-do spirit, entrepreneurial innovation, collaborative teamwork, the sense of service, and deep reverence for nature's ways that bring us safely to a renewable standard of living. Temperate needs, slower growth, and appropriate scale, coupled with modest returns on investment, will become the responsible means of doing business when nature becomes a partner rather than just a "resource" to exploit.

Grab this book and a friend or two, and head to the woods for a few days of study, hiking, and brainstorming. Explore what you are good at, what you love doing, who you love and want to work with, and then come back ready to make it happen no matter what.

If necessity,
mother of invention,
begs for creative release,
but doesn't know how . . .
the book is here
and your time is now . . .
Have at it!

DAVE SMITH

A BETTER WAY TO MAKE A LIVING

NOW what are you going to do?

Now what am I going to do? This is the question that nearly everyone I know, and everyone I have worked with, has asked at various times in their lives and careers. For most people, the question is asked and goes unanswered—we end up taking the first job that comes along, and we're usually disappointed or appalled at the result.

When I was a new graduate, I asked this question, fearful that my high expectations for finding meaningful work might never be realized. I asked it again a few months later when I had sent out more than two hundred résumés and applications and failed to get even one interview:

Now what am I going to do?

Today, when I speak to graduating classes in MBA and business-school programs, I hear the same question, and sense the same trepidation in our new graduates. The cattle call awaits them, and then the long climb to the top in organizations that, overwhelmingly, put profit ahead of the well-being of people, communities, and the environment. These students are filled with foreboding and dread. Even high school students sense it, and many will go to university for as long as possible just to delay having to answer this terrible question:

Now what am I going to do?

Later, when I was in my fifties, having bailed out of a career that was very successful financially but which left me feeling empty inside, I asked this question again. Like most Baby Boomers changing gears late in their careers, I tried the independent consultant route, doing what I'd been trained to do, but what I'd been trained to do wasn't what I *wanted* to do.

And I discovered a whole generation of my peers, in the last decade before they would supposedly retire, nearly one-fourth of the entire working-age population, looking for what are euphemistically called "second careers" to tide them over until they could actually afford to retire. Then, they hoped, they would finally get to do the things they really wanted to do. They were all asking the same question:

Now what am I going to do?

I have met hundreds of chronically underemployed people caught between the apprehensive young graduates chasing them up the ladder and the jaded and bewildered Boomers who are blocking their career advancement because they can't afford to retire.

I estimate that this chronically underemployed cohort makes up as much as half of the entire workforce—people longing to do work that is more satisfying, more joyful, less exhausting, more meaningful. And they, too, are asking, hopefully:

Now what am I going to do?

Throughout my career as an advisor to entrepreneurs and aspiring entrepreneurs, I have been studying those rare people who have found answers to this question. These are people who love getting up in the morning and going to work. These are people who don't work especially hard, or especially long hours. And they don't see what they do as "work" at all.

These are people whose work is completely aligned with their personal values, who are doing what they do best, working with people they love, whose skills mesh perfectly with their own.

These are people who never have to sell or market anything— their customers do their selling for them. These are people beholden to no one—not to bankers, shareholders, unreasonable customers, landlords, or creditors.

These are people who fall asleep easily every night, worry-free, with smiles on their faces, and wake up the same way, full of energy. These are people who have discovered a better, more natural way to make a living.

This book is about them, and how they did it, and about how, if

MEET THREE PROSPECTIVE NATURAL ENTREPRENEURS

Throughout this book, we're going to track the journey of three people asking the question: *Now what am I going to do?* We will follow them from the decision to become Natural Entrepreneurs to the creation, together, of a joyful, meaningful, sustainable, responsible business. They are composites of the three main categories of people who are asking this question, the people this book is meant for. They are:

Morgana, **not yet employed**, educated as an environmental journalist, is worried about global warming, and has a knack for understanding complex systems. After doing mostly volunteer intern work after graduating from high school, she went to business school "to learn something more practical." Unfortunately, she didn't learn anything practical. She's just graduated, still freelancing, and wondering what to do next.

Jean-Paul, **second-career seeker**, a social worker, wants to help the people of the world's struggling nations, and wants to show the young people of the world why he cares so much. After nearly thirty years of work, he's burned out, tired of not being able to make a difference. He's always worked for bureaucratic organizations and wants to strike out on his own, but isn't sure where to begin.

Janis, **underemployed**, mid-career, an engineer, is an inventor who wants to find ways to help the world address what she sees as a coming energy crisis as the world runs out of oil. She's worked as an assayer for oil companies for most of her career, unappreciated, overlooked, unable to find work doing what she is good at doing and what she cares about.

you're patient and willing to invest some time in the process, *you can do it, too.* So you won't ever have to ask again:

Now what am I going to do?

Because you'll already be doing it.

Here are some more dismaying data,[1] from Paul Craig Roberts, former U.S. Assistant Secretary to the Treasury, that tell us what the promised "information economy" and "creative economy" are actually yielding:

- In the past five years, U.S. manufacturing lost 2.9 million jobs, almost 17 percent of the manufacturing workforce. The wipe-out is across the board. Not a single manufacturing payroll classification created a single new job.

- Communications equipment lost 43 percent of its workforce. Semiconductors and electronic components lost 37 percent of its workforce. The workforce in computers and electronic products declined 30 percent. Electrical equipment and appliances lost 25 percent of its employees. The workforce in motor vehicles and parts declined 12 percent. Furniture and related products lost 17 percent of its jobs. Apparel manufacturers lost almost half of their workforce. Employment in textile mills declined 43 percent. Paper and paper products lost one-fifth of its jobs. The workforce in plastics and rubber products declined by 15 percent.

- The knowledge jobs that were supposed to take the place of lost manufacturing jobs in the globalized "new economy" never appeared. The information sector lost 17 percent of its jobs, with the telecommunications workforce declining by 25 percent. Even wholesale and retail trade lost jobs. Despite massive new accounting burdens imposed by Sarbanes-Oxley, accounting and bookkeeping employment shrank by 4 percent. Computer systems design and related lost 9 percent of its jobs. Today there are 209,000 *fewer* managerial and supervisory jobs than five years ago. There are several hundred thousand American engineers who are unemployed and have been for years. Offshore

WHY WE NEED A BETTER WAY

[*For Morgana's cohorts: the not yet employed*] We need to create 165,000 net new jobs per month in North America just to offset new immigration, graduation, layoffs, and plant closings. The Fortune 500 are creating none: Their hires of the young and inexpensive are almost exactly offset by layoffs, offshoring, deferred retirements, and outsourcing of costlier jobs. That means small and new enterprises now have to create all the net new jobs in our economy. We have no choice. For our recent graduates, new immigrants, and displaced workers, we must find an alternative to a life of wage slavery.

[*For Jean-Paul's cohorts: second-career seekers*] One-fourth of the entire North American workforce is now within a decade of retirement age. Nearly half of them have *already* conceded they won't have sufficient funds to retire when they leave their present jobs. Many of them will be facing—or are already facing—outsourcing, offshoring, downsizing, or early retirement in favor of cheaper young or overseas workers. Most of them have no idea what to do next. A lot of them hope to find more meaningful work in their "second careers," on their own terms.

[*For Janis's cohorts: the chronically underemployed*] Half of all North American workers assess themselves as underemployed. They're working at a job (or two, or three) below or *far* below their capabilities. Part-time work. Temporary work. Boring work. Meaningless work. Shift work. Work no one else wants to do—for a reason. A colossal waste of talent and passion. All because most of us have never learned how to make a living for ourselves.

outsourcing and offshore production have left the United States
awash with unemployment among the highly educated.

- The total number of private-sector jobs created during the last
  five-year period is less than one-eighth the net immigration
  during that period.

And here's a chart from the U.S. Department of Labor saying where
current "job growth" is occurring:

That adds up to hundreds of millions of people, all looking at a
stagnant, uninteresting, humiliating, fiercely competitive job market.
There are not enough jobs to go around, and most of the new jobs
are mundane, soul-destroying, and pay less than a living wage. We
can't go on like this.

If you're looking for a better way to making a living, you're not
alone.

There is a better way

I've spent the better part of my work life helping entrepreneurs
succeed. It's enormously satisfying work, and it has also given me the
opportunity to understand why so many people continue to tread
the dreadful traditional path of wage slavery, either as an employee
or as a beleaguered, struggling entrepreneur.

Because there is a better way.

I call it "working naturally," and I call the organizations that
embrace it "Natural Enterprises."
It's taken me a lifetime to grasp the
processes behind working naturally
and Natural Enterprises, because
the books and courses on business
and entrepreneurship and mapping
out your career don't talk about them.

> Books and courses on business, entrepreneurship, and mapping out your career don't talk about the processes behind working naturally.

Instead, these books and courses rehash the deeply entrenched
myths about work—the need to work hard, to sacrifice, to take great

Percent Change in Employment in Occupations Projected to Grow Fastest, 2004–2014, per U.S. Department of Labor

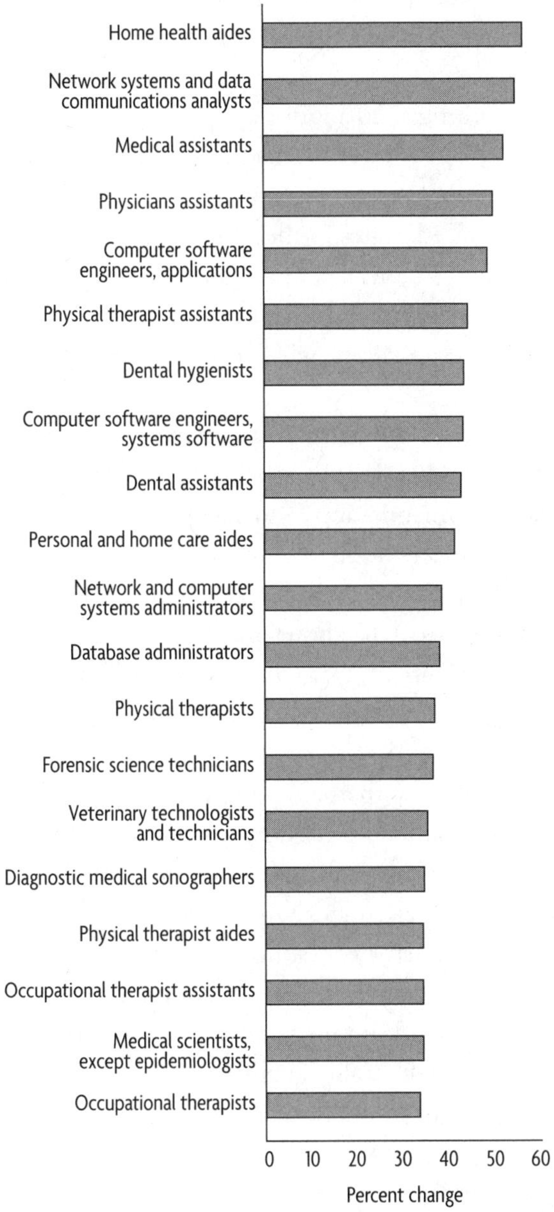

Home health aides	
Network systems and data communications analysts	
Medical assistants	
Physicians assistants	
Computer software engineers, applications	
Physical therapist assistants	
Dental hygienists	
Computer software engineers, systems software	
Dental assistants	
Personal and home care aides	
Network and computer systems administrators	
Database administrators	
Physical therapists	
Forensic science technicians	
Veterinary technologists and technicians	
Diagnostic medical sonographers	
Physical therapist aides	
Occupational therapist assistants	
Medical scientists, except epidemiologists	
Occupational therapists	

0   10   20   30   40   50   60

Percent change

risks if you want to get ahead, to work your way up, to be indebted to others, to manage horrific stress, to grow or die.

You *can* succeed, financially at least, that way. It's a way that takes a great personal toll. For more and more people, it's not worth it. And you don't have to do any of these things to succeed *on your own terms.*

When I started working as an advisor to entrepreneurs, I did it the traditional way. I developed some specialized skills. (I'm a Chartered Accountant in Canada, the equivalent of a Certified Public Accountant in the United States.) I became an expert accountant, auditor, tax advisor, and financial transaction specialist, working for my clients on IPOs, mergers and acquisitions, purchase investigations, refinancing and recapitalization of companies, and turnaround work.

But I've always been a voracious reader, and intensely curious about what works, and what doesn't, and why. I've also been blessed with a great, practical imagination, and have learned a great deal about the art of innovation and its role in successful enterprises.

I started inviting my clients to have an extended breakfast with me, once a quarter, just to talk about and learn more about their businesses. To my astonishment, I discovered I had as much to teach them, far outside my narrow areas of professional specialty, as I had to learn.

This is because, after more than a decade working with hundreds of entrepreneurial clients, I had picked up a lot of knowledge about what worked (success stories—success being on the clients' own terms) and what didn't (war stories with important lessons). I was often able to recount these stories (without violating confidentiality, of course) to other clients facing similar situations.

In addition, because I read so much and was always curious about how to solve problems, I had also acquired the ability to transfer knowledge I'd picked up from my readings and apply it in an entirely different context.

So, for example, one day I had been reading about how the color in butterflies' wings is not due to pigment (which would weigh too

Scanning electron micrograph of a butterfly wing. ©TINA CARVALHO/MICROANGELA.

much for the tiny butterfly to support), but rather due to refraction—the way the cells of the wing were layered to reflect light.

When I spoke to a client in the thin-film coatings business later that day, at one of our quarterly breakfasts, I asked him whether this might have some application in his industry. As we kicked the idea around, he became very animated about the potential use of this "technology" in anticounterfeiting of banknotes, and in "painting" aircraft (where paint weight can significantly reduce fuel mileage).

I later learned that this application of natural "technologies" to human use is called *biomimicry*, and Janine Benyus has written a wonderful book about it.[2]

Eventually, these quarterly breakfasts became so valuable to my clients (and to me) that some clients told me that they'd be willing to pay more for them than for all the statutory accounting and tax work I did for them.

At that point I knew that I was on to something. I had to share this knowledge—what I'd learned from my clients that could be applied to other industries, and the value of innovation that starts with applying learning from one discipline, or from nature, to an entirely different one—with other entrepreneurs and entrepreneurs-to-be.

I continued to study entrepreneurs who seemed almost to defy gravity—work for them was just easier, more fun, less stressful than entrepreneurship was *supposed* to be.

What I was learning was that most of the myths about entrepreneurial success are just wrong, and that the most exciting enterprises had stumbled upon a more natural way to make a living. None of these "joyful" companies had discovered the *entire* secret to Natural Enterprise, but each of them offered a part of a better answer.

Eventually, the six key steps to natural entrepreneurship started to fall into place.

This book tells you what they are.

What's holding you back?

The Ten Fears of Entrepreneurship

1. Don't Have the Skills
2. Don't Have the Self-Confidence
3. Don't Have the Ideas
4. Don't Have the Money
5. The Deck's Stacked Against Entrepreneurs
6. Couldn't Handle the Failure
7. Don't Know the Process
8. Don't Have the Time
9. Couldn't Handle the Stress
10. Couldn't Handle the Loneliness

I had the chance a few months ago to speak informally with a group of young people (in their twenties and thirties) about whether they would ever consider starting their own business. They had been grousing about their dead-end jobs, asshole bosses, 9-to-5 (and sometimes two-job) boredom, and how desperately they looked forward to the weekend.

When I probed a bit about finding or creating meaningful work, most of them said that they didn't think any "existing" job would let them do the kind of work they really loved or were really suited to doing.

And although they liked the idea of starting their own enterprise, they were uniformly dismissive of the possibility of actually doing so, and confessed to being afraid to do so, to the point most of them said they would never even seriously consider it.

I made notes of their reasons, which I've dubbed "The ten fears of entrepreneurship." Here they are, along with my explanation of why their fears are unwarranted, and how working naturally can overcome them:

> **1. Don't Have the Skills:** "I wouldn't know where to start. I took entrepreneurship in college, but it was all about understanding financial statements and types of loans. I've never even spoken to a successful entrepreneur."

This fear comes from the belief that entrepreneurs need to know it all and have it all. The Natural Enterprises I know understand that just as it takes a village to raise a child, it takes a "community" of diverse people with different skills to make a business work. The tragedy is that the most critical skills needed for natural work are capacities that are intuitive and inherent, not specialized skills you need to study. The greater tragedy is that our education system doesn't help us recognize what our natural talents and capacities are. Most of us need to learn what these are ourselves.

> **2. Don't Have the Self-Confidence:** "I'd get discouraged too early in the process. It all sounds so intimidating. You have to have nerves of steel and incredible courage to take this on. I know some entrepreneurs, and I don't envy them."

Entrepreneurship needn't be intimidating. It is mostly fear of the unknown, and the lingering mythology of entrepreneurship that is perpetuated, alas, because so many entrepreneurs keep making the same avoidable mistakes over and over. Working naturally, doing what you love doing and do well, is, well, *natural*.

3. Don't Have the Ideas: "I'm not creative enough to come up with something novel. Entrepreneurs have these great ideas, and even then it's not always enough to make a new business work."

Perception, not conception, is the key to entrepreneurial success: Paying attention is far more important than creativity. It's all about finding a need and filling it, not coming up with an idea, "commercializing" it, and then trying to find someone who might buy it.

4. Don't Have the Money: "If I had another ten grand, it would go to paying debts or meeting other immediate needs, not investing in a risky new business. And I'm not foolish enough to think anyone else would give me the money, either."

If you can fill an unmet need, there are several ways to finance the business organically, drawing on the interest and investment capital of suppliers, potential customers, and business partners, and people you know who are always looking for a way of getting a better return than they can get in the bank.

5. The Deck's Stacked Against Entrepreneurs: "Big corporations have all the money, the subsidies from government, the tax breaks, and the cash to intimidate, sue, or buy out any entrepreneur who challenges their dominance."

There is some truth to this, which is why the key to successful entrepreneurship is to find a need that is not immediately or obviously big enough or profitable enough to attract the attention of the dominant players in your industry. This is what Clay Christensen calls Disruptive Innovation, and entrepreneurs have the advantage of agility (and not having shareholders demanding seven-digit revenues from any new offering) that makes them more adept at doing this than large corporations. This ability to innovate, as I'll explain in detail later, is a great equalizer.

6. Couldn't Handle the Failure: "If I tried and failed as an entrepreneur, I think I'd be crushed. I'd feel like a failure in life, it would probably affect my marriage and my friendships and my reputation, and if I came to hate my day job, I wouldn't even be able to daydream about running my own business, because I'd have already tried that and failed."

A survey a few years ago by *Inc.* magazine found that only one factor correlated strongly with entrepreneurial success: A *previous entrepreneurial failure. This is how you learn.* If you avoid overcommitting, and learn how to "fail fast and early," you can have the resilience to be a "serial entrepreneur." No entrepreneur succeeds in every undertaking. Natural entrepreneurs don't have to.

7. Don't Know the Process: "I took some MBA courses, and they didn't teach me anything about how to start or run my own business. Where do you learn this?"

This is the principal function of this book. But although the book lays out the process, applying it depends on the nature of the enterprise you are undertaking. Learning how to apply it comes from spending time with other entrepreneurs, and drawing on the experience and knowledge of your business partners, and advisors. *Most people love to see new enterprises succeed, and those who can help are usually very generous with their time and counsel.*

8. Don't Have the Time: "I'm working two jobs now just to make ends meet. If there were more hours in the week, I'd take a third one. How could I ever find the time to start my own business?"

The biggest time-consumer in starting a successful Natural Enterprise is the up-front research. But that research can be done while you're doing other things you're already committed to. Social occasions, courses, shopping trips, sales calls, dinners out, even watching your kids' after-school activities—all of these are opportunities to observe, explore, and research untapped needs that could be the basis for a successful entrepreneurial venture. Take your time, do your research well, share the workload with your entrepreneurial partners. You'll then be so sure of success that you'll be able to confidently make the time to bring your business idea to fruition.

> **9. Couldn't Handle the Stress:** "The entrepreneurs I know are in hock to the bank or to demanding investors, their personal assets are at stake, their families depend on them for steady income, and a single bad debt or overrun could sink them. Life's too short for that much stress."

Entrepreneurs who live with that much daily stress (and there are a lot of them) are, in my experience, mostly running ill-conceived businesses. I know many entrepreneurs who absolutely love their work, are beholden to no one, and are doing so well they can afford to turn away lots of business (especially from aggravating customers) because they'd rather pursue leisure activities than work long hours. If your business truly taps an unmet need, you'll have good customers, and very little business stress.

> **10. Couldn't Handle the Loneliness:** "The entrepreneurs I know are the loneliest people in the world. They work incredible hours and have no time for anything else. They have to learn how to do everything themselves, because they can't afford experts and consultants."

The biggest mistake a lot of people make in starting their own business is trying to do it all themselves. One-person enterprises have the highest rate of failure, largely because *no one* can know everything you need to know, or have all the requisite skills, to succeed in business. One of the most critical decisions in creating a Natural Enterprise is finding business partners who have skills and knowledge that complement (without overlapping) your own, who have the same commitment to the idea that you do, and who you love working with. Get that right, and how could you possibly be lonely?

Recently I've heard an eleventh fear, or objection, from progressives and environmentalists: They don't believe business can be socially and environmentally responsible, ethical, and responsive to needs beyond financial demands for "return on investment."

At some point, they say, every business starts to compromise its principles, and goes from being part of the solution to being part of the problem. This perception comes, I think, from the fact that the largest and most visible corporations, including those that start with responsible ideals and values, are beholden to shareholders and investors. As Joel Bakan argues in his book *The Corporation*,[3] the very structure and charter of corporations make them inherently pathological, and driven by the market's demand for profit and a large return on investment to grow ever larger.

Most Natural Enterprises are not corporations, and they don't need or aspire to grow. In Charles Handy's book *The Age of Paradox*,[4] Handy interviews the natural entrepreneur who owns a top-rated winery in California:

> After one sun-drenched day in the wine country of California, I asked the owner of the winery about the future. He was passionate about their winery, he said; they were putting back every cent they could into its growth. "Where can you grow?" I asked, looking around at the valley where every inch of land was now fully planted with other people's vines. "Oh, we don't want to expand," he said, "we want to grow *better*, not bigger."

In the foreword to this book, Dave Smith explains how some of his entrepreneurial ventures succeeded naturally, while others, beholden to corporate shareholders, compromised their values of responsibility, quality, and sustainability and, in Dave's view, became "failures."

The natural form of enterprise is a nonhierarchical partnership that measures success in its own terms—the collective objectives of its partners, including social and environmental responsibility, sustainability, and the ability, in Dave Smith's words, *to be of use.*

> The natural form of enterprise is a nonhierarchical partnership that measures success in its own terms–the collective objectives of its partners, including social and environmental responsibility, sustainability, and the ability to be of use.

Such enterprises grow better, not bigger. Not only do they not compromise the ideals of their partners of responsibility to each other, to their communities, and to the Earth, our ability to create such enterprises to supplant the pathological corporations that are ravaging our planet is essential to the very survival of our planet and the well-being of our children and grandchildren.

Not only is there a better way to make a living, it is central to our species finding a better way to live.

Can't be much more responsible than that. And doesn't the idea of doing so give you the courage to work past the ten fears of entrepreneurship?

Recently, our local television news told the story of Lucky, a dog whose life started out badly, but turned out just fine. Lucky (so named by the Humane Society when they rescued him) was left behind when the family of an alcoholic and abusive man fled to a social services shelter, a "halfway house" that didn't allow dogs.

Neighbors say Lucky was beaten several times by this man, and left outside in all weather, but steadfastly refused to run away, and even came back to more abuse after the man told neighbors that he'd driven the dog a mile away and abandoned him.

What earned Lucky his name was his discovery, a month later, flailing weakly in a country ditch fifty miles away, by a caring couple who found him, bruised, emaciated, feet tied together, and nearly dead. Nursed back to health by the Humane Society with the help of an outpouring of local donations from citizens, Lucky had more than a hundred adoption offers.

The reporters covering the story raised the issue of why Lucky didn't run away, and kept coming back for more abuse from this man. They used the words "brave" and "loyal" to describe this behavior. It obviously didn't occur to the reporters that Lucky came back for more abuse because *that's the only life he knew.* He couldn't have survived in the wild, and couldn't have known that another, better life was waiting for him in just about any other house, with any other family.

We are all, in a real sense, like Lucky. Most of us, all over the world, struggle every day, and put up with a huge amount of stress and unhappiness in our lives.

Compared to the hunter-gatherers who lived a natural life for millions of years before modern civilization, we work much harder[5] and longer to make a living. We face much more physical and psychological violence (in our neighborhoods, in our workplaces, in our war-torn world, and sometimes even in our homes).

We suffer from many more physical and psychological diseases, we live in crowded, polluted, mostly run-down communities, in constant fear (of an infinite number of things, most notably not having enough), and we are oppressed with hierarchies, laws, rules, and restrictions that would have driven our ancient ancestors quite mad.

Why do we put up with it? Because *it's the only life we know.*

It has always struck me as odd that wild creatures on this planet look after the needs of their community before their individual needs. This is natural to them. The "dog-eat-dog" world is ours, not theirs! And hunter-gatherer cultures even today live leisurely lives compared to ours, and seem much happier with their natural way of living and making a living.

I believe it's because of the brainwashing we get in the education system, in the workplace, in the media, and in society at large, that we think the lifelong, often joyless and meaningless struggle in the workplace is the only way to make a living.

We should know better. Just because it's the only way we know how to make a living doesn't mean it is the only way. There is a better way. The only thing holding most of us back is lacking the knowledge of that way. This book will give you that knowledge.

Do you have what it takes?

I've learned that you don't need an MBA to be a great entrepreneur (in some ways MBAs who are taught the myths of entrepreneurship are at a disadvantage compared to "uneducated" entrepreneurs), but in my experience there are twelve essential capacities for entrepreneurship, and some essential knowledge. You may be surprised at them—they're capacities most of us are born with, although the education system may beat them out of us by the time we're ready to make a living for ourselves. You don't have to have all of them yourself, but when you're looking for enterprise partners (Chapter 2), you should be looking for these capacities in them, to make sure that, between you and your partners, you have them covered, and know who's most competent at each.

Here are the twelve capacities:

> **Excellent instincts:** A subconscious ability to sense what is going right and wrong, when you're being told the truth, and not, and what is happening that is not being expressed in words, data, or written reports. This is close to the concept called "emotional intelligence." It is a capacity that can be honed, but mostly we all have it; we just need to be aware of it, and trust it.
>
> **Critical-thinking skills:** The ability to think logically, to assess information and opinions intelligently, to extract and convey insight, to "make sense" of it. This is a learnable skill, but one that some people are just naturally better at than others. You need to know which of your partners have this ability, and trust them to exercise it to your collective advantage.
>
> **Imaginative skills:** The ability to conjure up, by putting different ideas

together, or out of nothing but pure imagination, what is possible, to address needs or problems that arise in the enterprise or are identified by customers or potential customers. Like critical thinking, this is a learnable skill that some people are just naturally better at than others.

Creative skills: These are different from imaginative skills, and are about the ability to make the abstract (ideas and imaginings) real, to bring them to life, to make them work in the real world given all of the constraints you must deal with. Like critical thinking and imagination, this is a learnable skill that some people are just naturally better at than others, but interestingly, the people with strong imaginative skills aren't always creative, and vice versa. Some people can create (or, like artists, *re*-create), what exists in another form or what others have imagined, but aren't good at imagining possibilities themselves. And some people with great imaginations lack the practical bent to envision how those ideas can be made real. You need both in your enterprise, and you will not necessarily find them in the same person.

Attention skills: The ability to see patterns, to scan broadly for ideas and events that could be important and bring them to others' attention, and also the ability to listen, watch, and focus the senses on perceiving what is really happening, and then, with your partners, assessing what it means.

Communication skills: The ability to articulate, orally and in writing, what you think, what you mean, what you intend, and why, and the ability to craft and relate *stories*. Stories are valuable because, unlike most of the raw data that is used in decision-making in traditional corporations, stories provide rich context and understanding, and are hence much more valuable for decision-making. Communication skills are different from *persuasive* skills, which, in my experience, are not essential in Natural Enterprises—because Natural Enterprises *respond* to needs, rather than trying to create them.

Demonstration skills: Showing people is usually more compelling than telling them, but demonstration is an art form that requires the demonstrator to put him- or herself in the position of the person watching, to anticipate questions and misunderstandings, and to see things from different perspectives. Good demonstrators are not charismatic, because personal charisma, while attractive, can actually detract from the effectiveness of communication.

Learning skills: Our education system is pretty poor at helping us learn how to learn. This ability is essential to entrepreneurial success, because every aspect of entrepreneurship entails continuous learning. This has more to do with openness than intellectual capacity. It's about an ability to let go of preconceptions and conceptions and be completely flexible to new ideas and information and possibilities, even if it contradicts what you thought you knew.

Responsibility: In traditional corporations, this is a "leadership" role. The people on the front line are often even discouraged from taking responsibility, because, as we learn in MBA school, responsibility and authority need to be matched. If you have responsibility without commensurate authority, you are likely to get stressed and quit. If you have authority without commensurate responsibility, you are likely to abuse (perhaps unintentionally, perhaps intentionally) that authority, to behave *irresponsibly*. In a Natural Enterprise, authority is shared and devolved. Each person has authority for decisions and actions that he or she is competent to make or perform, provided they are not complex or controversial. The partners collectively have the authority for complex and controversial decisions and actions, those requiring consensus. So in Natural Enterprises, each partner must be personally responsible for his or her personal decisions and actions, and accept collective responsibility for complex or controversial decisions and actions. That collective responsibility means not saying, later, "I never thought that was a good idea, I just didn't say anything because the rest of you had your minds made up." In the larger sense, responsibility also entails accepting responsibility for the well-being of your partners, as you and they have collectively defined well-being.

Self-management: Self-management is the natural extension of responsibility. Personal self-management entails self-knowledge, exercising authority as appropriate, seeking consensus as appropriate, and accepting responsibility. It is also about holistically "looking after" yourself—staying healthy and positive, continuously learning, identifying what capacities you have, which you would like to develop, and which you are not strong at, and behaving accordingly, and prudently. And the enterprise as a whole needs to learn to self-manage collectively. This is a capacity that we all have innately, but many of us who are used to working in hierarchical organizations may be unpracticed at it. It takes continuous practice, which fortunately Natural Enterprise provides lots of!

Passion: This starts with your personal Passion, and with the opportunity to apply that passion to your Purpose (these concepts are described in Chapter 1). But it extends also to your partners—you need to be passionate about them as well. Love is not too strong a word to apply to the level of emotional connection that partners in Natural Enterprise need to have with each other. You need to care not only for what you are doing in the enterprise but also for what the enterprise as a whole is doing, and for what your partners care about.

Collaboration: Although traditional corporations talk a good story about collaboration, and have "collaboration software," most of what people do together in those organizations is really just coordination and cooperation. Most work tasks are parceled out to individuals and done by individuals. Although there is certainly some individual work in a Natural Enterprise, much if not most of the work is truly collaborative—it entails people doing work together, producing work product that is collective and cannot be identified as the work of any individual, and, most important, achieving results greater than those that any the people in the organization, working individually, could possibly have achieved. This is discussed in more detail in Chapter 6.

In addition to these capacities, prospective Natural Entrepreneurs need to understand the new economy and how it differs from the industrial economy. Most businesspeople (including entrepreneurs) have not had the time or inclination to keep up with the important changes to our economy that new technology and the Internet in particular are bringing about. And most traditional business education is behind the curve on understanding these changes as well.

There is a growing consensus that the prevailing industrial economy is unsustainable and dysfunctional. Although the corporate giants would like us to believe it is a "free market" economy, the immense disparity of wealth and power in the twenty-first century, and the cynical use of that wealth and power to perpetuate the control of oligopolies (small groups of very large companies in each industry in our economy that conspire to fix prices and reduce competition), have produced massive distortions in an economy that ostensibly matches suppliers' goods, services, and prices to customers' needs, wants, and the perceived value of those goods and services.

In addition, the industrial economy thrives by "externalizing" (shifting to taxpayers or to other nations with low wages and low social and environmental standards) its costs, instead of being responsible for them. This has produced terrible dislocation for workforces in affluent nations; working conditions akin to slavery and utter environmental devastation and resource exhaustion in struggling nations; and the pollution, global warming, chronic poverty, violence, and other consequences of that irresponsibility.

A new group of economists, people such as Herman Daly and Richard Douthwaite, are mapping the transition of the industrial economy to a new, more resilient economy. The Internet is a significant catalyst for this transformation, because it allows more untrammeled exchange of information and knowledge and because it enables more connectivity of potential business partners looking for new, more-effective business models. Already we are seeing the emergence of open-source development of new products and new markets, and methods of building relationships, creating ventures, and conducting business that are not constrained by oligopoly.

The resource guide at the end of this book includes information about where to find a short series of essays explaining why the industrial economy is unsustainable and beginning to decline, and describing some of the emerging new ways of doing business, and the new economy that is beginning to form around them, an economy that has been variously described as a "World of Ends" economy, a postindustrial economy, and a network economy. Whatever it is called, this new economy will make it easier for Natural Enterprises to form, collaborate, and succeed with their customers. However it continues to evolve, it will be a more "natural" economy.

An understanding of how the business world really works and how it is changing requires a continuous investment in environmental scanning and in learning. Although some of it can be done online (or by reading books like this), a more-profound and effective understanding requires wearing out some shoe leather—visiting with other entrepreneurs to observe how they are evolving as the new economy emerges, to see how they are coping with complexity and building resilience, and to learn what works and what doesn't.

This is one reason why I discourage entrepreneurs from trying to do everything themselves—no one person has time to run a business and to keep abreast of what's changing.

The six steps to Natural Entrepreneurship

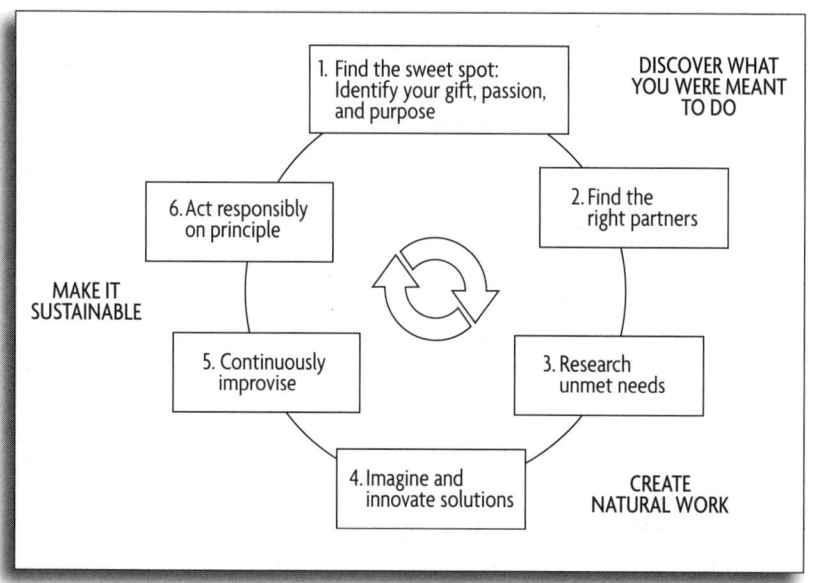

The Natural Entrepreneur is a book in three parts. The first part, **Discovering What You Were Meant to Do**, describes the process of discovering for yourself what you were *meant* to do, and with whom.

> **Finding the Sweet Spot** introduces the concepts of our Gift (what we do uniquely well), our Passion (what we love to do), and our Purpose (what is needed), and presents an iterative, collaborative process for finding their intersection—natural work. It addresses the question: *What am I meant to do?*
>
> **Finding the Right Partners** explains the need for and process of discovering business partners with complementary skills. It escalates the identification of one's *personal* Gift, Passion, and Purpose to the identification of your enterprise's *collective* Gifts, Passions, and Purpose. The message is that the most successful, joyful, and sustainable enterprises are collective and egalitarian, and that "going it alone" is rarely a wise entrepreneurial strategy. It addresses the question: *Who should I make a living with?*

The second part of the book, **Creating Natural Work**, shows how to apply the knowledge of the fledgling enterprise's personal and collective Gifts, Passions, and Purpose, and the principles of Natural Entrepreneurship, to new business creation.

Finding Unmet Needs to Fill is about the process of performing rigorous market research, using some established and some new and promising techniques to identify unmet needs that you *know* your enterprise can effectively provide, and hence reduce the risk of enterprise failure to almost zero. It addresses the question: *What does the world need?*

Imagining and Innovating Solutions shows how collective imagination can transform identified needs to ideas, and presents a process to convert these ideas to practical innovations, and realize them, and explains how innovation shifts competitive advantage from established big businesses to creative entrepreneurs. It addresses the question: *What could possibly meet that need?*

The third part of the book, **Making It Sustainable**, describes the principles, values, infrastructure, and modus operandi that distinguish Natural Enterprises from traditional corporations, and why they are so important.

The Resilience of Natural Enterprise explains why Natural Enterprises are very different from traditional enterprises, debunks the common myths of entrepreneurship, and explores how Natural Entrepreneurs improvise and adapt instead of trying to plan and "manage" risks. It addresses the question: *How do we adapt to change?*

The Power of People explains the importance and power of responsibility, collaboration, relationships, and community—the human connection that further distinguishes Natural Enterprises from traditional corporations. It addresses the question: *How should we behave?*

The book concludes with "next steps" to help you learn more about Natural Entrepreneurship, and get you started turning the ideas in this book into reality.

The six steps outlined in these six chapters define a *holistic, integral* approach to enterprise creation. They are all essential to Natural Enterprise success, and they work best when they're implemented together.

A process and a collaboration, not just a book

No book can, by itself, give you everything you need to decide what kind of work you were meant to do, or everything you need to succeed as an entrepreneur.

Chelsea Green is hosting three collaborative tools that complement *The Natural Entrepreneur* on the book's Web site, tools that will allow natural entrepreneurs to find, work with, and help each other.

I will be active in facilitating this ongoing process and future editions of this book will present success stories and a refined Natural Enterprise model as, together, we continue to discover what works.

The three tools are:

Finding Natural Partners [http://NaturalEnterprise.org/partners/]—This is a social-networking tool that allows you to write about your Gift, your Passion, and your Purpose (these concepts are explained in Chapter 1), and find partners with complementary abilities and shared values and life goals.

The Natural Enterprise Community [http://NaturalEnterprises.org/community]—This is a venue for sharing your success (on your own terms) stories, war stories, challenges, and advice with other natural entrepreneurs. "Experts" may chime in, but experience suggests the most valuable advice comes freely from those who have faced similar issues themselves in their own enterprises.

The Natural Collaboratory [http://NaturalEnterprise.org/collaboratory]—This is an idea market with a difference. The only investments in this "market" are your time, energy, and enthusiasm. No money changes hands and no "selling" is permitted. This is a place to:

- Float ideas,
- Do some secondary research,
- Get the "crowd" of prospective customers and coworkers to tell you what they think, and
- Work collaboratively to bring ideas to light and then to fruition.

The journey to Natural Entrepreneurship starts with yourself, as every important change starts with self-change and self-discovery. The first chapter will challenge you to discover your Gift (what you do uniquely well), your Passion (what you love doing), and your Purpose (what you're meant to do, applying that Gift and Passion to what is needed).

Fasten your seatbelt. Here we go.

PART ONE

DISCOVERING WHAT YOU WERE MEANT TO DO

FINDING THE SWEET SPOT
where your gifts, your passions, and your purpose intersect

What do people really want? They want to find work they're passionate about. Offering benefits and incentives are mere compromises. Educating people is important but not enough. We need to encourage people to find their sweet spot. Productivity explodes when people love what they do.

—Po Bronson, *What Should I Do With My Life?*[1]

Every one of us knows what our purpose is. It is only ever a question of how long it takes to articulate it.

—Neil Crofts, *Authentic Business*[2]

The sweet spot, and why it's so hard to find

A couple of years ago, Dick Richards published a book called *Is Your Genius at Work?: Four Questions to Ask Before Your Next Career Move.*[3] It was designed for people contemplating (or forced into) a job change, and was especially valuable for those lacking self-confidence—those who don't believe they *have* a "genius," those who don't believe they are especially good at anything.

Dick's approach also can be useful for helping entrepreneurs and aspiring entrepreneurs decide what kind of enterprise they might be interested in working in, or founding. To this end, I separated what he calls "Genius" into two components:

- Your Gifts: What you're uniquely good at—what you do better than *anyone* else, and
- Your Passions: What you love doing

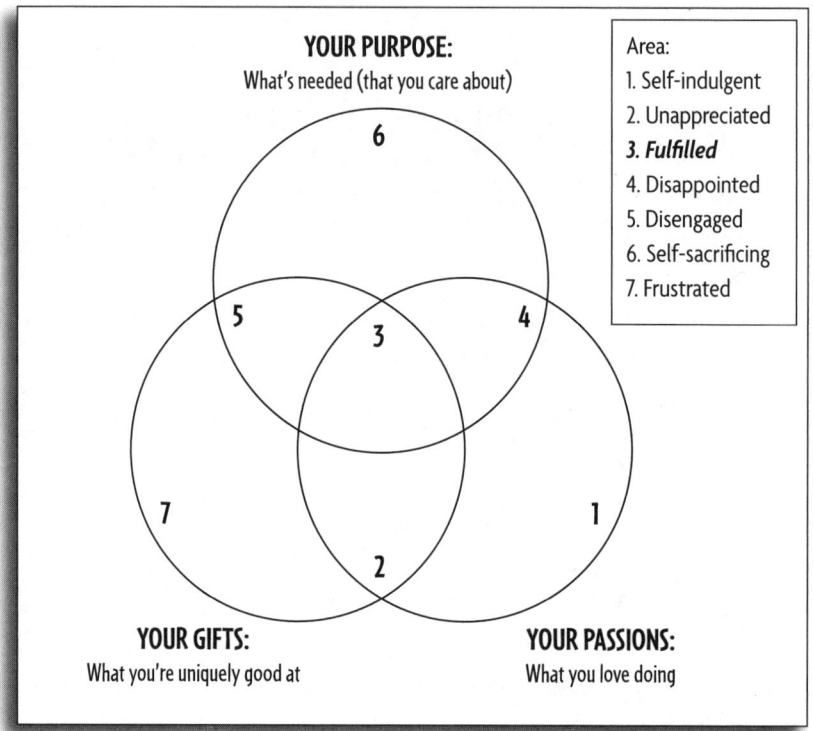

YOUR PURPOSE:
What's needed (that you care about)

Area:
1. Self-indulgent
2. Unappreciated
3. *Fulfilled*
4. Disappointed
5. Disengaged
6. Self-sacrificing
7. Frustrated

YOUR GIFTS:
What you're uniquely good at

YOUR PASSIONS:
What you love doing

Finding what you were meant to do is about finding where your Gifts and your Passions intersect with what is needed.

As the chart above shows, finding what you were meant to do is about finding where your Gifts and your Passions intersect with what is needed—with a few caveats:

- Your Gifts have to be recognized—acknowledged by prospective customers as being something you are uniquely good at. As many artists, scientists, and inventors can tell you, it is possible to be too far ahead of the market. It's also possible to be self-deluded about your talents.
- Your Gifts have to be appreciated by prospective customers as having value. If speaking fluent Klingon is your Gift, this could be a problem!
- Your Passions have to have enough perceived value that customers will pay for them. Without this, your enterprise partners will

have to subsidize you. If they love you enough, they may be willing to do this. Or they may not!

- You must have enough time to pursue your Passion, to develop it to the point that it is marketable. When it comes to our Passions, we may be inclined to spend more time on them than is warranted.
- The need that you offer to fill must be recognized as such by prospective customers. You may think there is a need for some new social software technology, but if it isn't recognized as such, it is doubtful that "marketing" will change that.
- The product or service you offer must be affordable by those who need it. As we've learned with the challenges of getting AIDS medicines to the world's struggling nations, those with the greatest needs often can least afford to pay for the products and services that meet those needs.
- You need to be able to circumvent bureaucracy and cultural obstacles to acceptance of your product or service. The "morning-after pill," for example, took years longer to become available (and is still less available than other medications) because of the ferocious political and cultural resistance to it from conservative and religious groups.

The process of finding the "sweet spot" is a challenging one. It may also be *iterative*—you may start with your Gifts, your Passions, or a need, and go back and forth many times between them before you discover where they intersect.

You may find that they don't intersect at all, perhaps for one of the reasons above. In that case, you may need to go back and reexplore what other Gifts you might have, or how your Gifts might be attuned to better meet a need or connect better with your Passions. Or you may have to learn more about Gifts or Passions you might have that have not yet been revealed. Or you may have to do some research to understand what needs may exist that you were not aware of.

To some extent, I think we all intuitively do this when we try to decide what we're going to do for a living. But we tend not to do it rigorously, for a number of reasons:

- We may not believe that we have much choice. Malcolm Gladwell describes[4] a phenomenon he calls Learned Helplessness—the "learning," from bitter experience, that we have no control over things, and that we need to wait for others to do things for us. In the case of looking for work, this means accepting that we must work for other people, do what we're told, and not expect much.

- We don't know much about the world of work. Our education system shelters us from, rather than exposing us to, what goes on in the workplace and in the economy at large. We learn about abstractions, and rarely visit real workplaces, and when we do, we don't really know what goes on there. In fact, it's likely that most of the people *working there* don't really know what goes on there, outside their immediate areas of responsibility!

- We don't know much about ourselves. Very few people are curious enough to try to discover what they are capable of. Many skills and capabilities are not tested in the school system or in most workplaces, so they remain latent, and we never find out about them.

- We lack the ability to imagine what's possible. Our education system seems very adept at driving the creativity and imagination out of us. So trying to imagine how our Gifts or Passions might be applied to meet some important human need is difficult for us—it's like exercising an unused muscle.

We could start with any of the three circles, but let's start with discovering our Gifts.

Your Gifts: What you do uniquely well

The word "gift" is an ancient Norse word that means something bestowed or endowed. I chose this word to describe the first circle of discovering what you were meant to do, deliberately, because it refers to both

- What you were given, your natural endowment of talent, and

- What you give to others, how you pass on what you were given.

With few exceptions, the people I have known throughout my life, entrepreneurs or not, don't really know what their Gifts are. They may know what they were good at in school. They may be aware of what they have been told they have done well in the workplace and in hobbies and recreational sports.

They may have undergone aptitude and interest tests to stream them in certain career directions. But they still don't know what their Gifts are. They don't know themselves that well. And they have not tried enough different things to learn what they are capable of.

But you have to start somewhere.

There are some who believe that your Gifts are things that you were predestined to do, a divine endowment, something absolutely and deliberately unique to you, just waiting to find realization.

My thinking on this is more prosaic: I believe societies whose members have diverse and complementary skills and talents thrive, and those that don't, don't. So I think the fact that we all have relatively unique Gifts, and a deep-seated natural desire to put them to use in service to others, has an adaptive rather than spiritual purpose—it has helped us to survive as a species.

I do believe, however, that the Gifts we are endowed with are natural and are intended to obtain natural expression in the work we do. When I speak of discovering what we were "meant" to do, I'm referring to this natural matching of talent and role in community-

> **The Gifts we are endowed with are natural and are intended to obtain natural expression in the work we do.**

based work, rather than something predestined. If it were predestined, surely fewer of us would be doing unnatural, boring, ill-suited, meaningless work!

I also believe that the greatest part of the challenge of finding the sweet spot is our ignorance of what our Gifts, our natural talents, things we do easily, are. We live in a world that is terribly specialized, and we are driven early in life to pick one of a few narrow career channels that are suited to the needs of today's large, impersonal, industrial employers, and to stop dreaming or thinking about doing anything else.

Here are a few questions to ponder when thinking about what your Gift or Gifts might be:

- What have people told you you are especially good at? What competencies allow you to be good at doing those things?
- What activities have you received the most praise for, in work or outside? What allowed you to achieve that praise? Did it come easily or was it hard won?
- What have you done, or tried to do, that was especially frustrating? What made it so difficult?
- What tasks come easiest to you, whether you enjoy them or not? What do people get you to do because they know you can do it quickly and simply?
- Intuitively, if someone asked you what your "natural talent" was, how would you answer?
- If you've taken aptitude tests, did they tell you at what you should excel?
- What did you get the best grades or scores in, in school, with the least work?
- What hobbies or recreational activities that you do, or have done, do you think (or have others suggested) you might be good enough to make a living at? Why?
- What do you, or others, consider your greatest accomplishments? Which of them came easily to you?
- What are you most capable working with: people, tools, ideas, or information?
- What do people most often seek you out and ask you to do? Which of those things have always been easy for you to do, and why?

I've often been asked: What is the difference between skills, talents, competencies, and Gifts?

A talent is an innate ability, while a skill is, generally, an acquired one.

The word "competence" comes from the same Latin root as the word "compete," but you may be surprised to know it doesn't mean "try to do better than." It means "to strive together"! So a competency, literally, is something that enables you to strive together with others to achieve a collective goal.

Competency presumes a combination of both talent and skill. And a Gift, as I use it (capitalized) in this book, is a relatively unique competency—one that is rare or unusually advanced. It is possible, with a lot of work, to develop a skill in an area in which you have no talent. And it is certainly possible to have a (latent) talent that is never applied. I think your Gift is a *natural* competency. It is one that comes easily to you, one that have a talent for *and* have found (or could easily find) an outlet for in your work or other activities. It is more than either a talent or a skill.

You may think you know intuitively what your Gift or Gifts are. Or you may have absolutely no idea. But it's time to start looking for the sweet spot, so turn to page 61 where there is a blank working copy of the three circles.

Thinking about the questions just posed, or what your instincts tell you, write in the Gift circle some of the things you think your Gift or Gifts might be, the things you believe you are, or could be, uniquely and naturally good at.

Don't try to think ahead to the sweet spot: Your Gift, your Passion, and your Purpose probably overlap somewhere, but at this point, I want you to focus *just* on your Gifts, what you do uniquely well. Don't discount them just because you have no Passion for them, or because you don't think there's a market for them. If they're your Gifts, they're your Gifts. In some respects, it's even more important to know what Gifts you have that *don't* overlap your Passions and your Purpose, because most of us face a lot of pressure and temptation to do what we're gifted at, even if we hate it or it's useless.

Don't worry if you're not sure what to write. The journey is just starting, and we'll come back to this soon. Later in this chapter we'll describe some examples of Gifts that various people have identified for themselves. And I'll tell you my own story and how I filled in and used the three circles to find my sweet spot. But I don't want you to be influenced by them yet.

Next step: Identifying your Passion.

Your Passions: What you love doing

The second of the natural work circles is your Passions. At first blush, identifying it might seem easier than identifying your Gift. But, just as a poverty of experience can prevent us from knowing our Gifts, it can prevent us knowing our Passions.

We might imagine that mountain-climbing or working for Google or working with a group delivering medicine to villages in struggling nations or teaching people to do something we do well might engage our passions, might be something we would love to do.

But as you probably have discovered, we often find that something we thought we would love turns out to be something we hate—most of us have dropped out of something that we were originally energized about at some point in our lives.

> There are many things that we have not done, or not even imagined doing that we might discover are what we love doing most of all.

On the flip side, there are many things that we have not done, or not even imagined doing, that we don't think we would like doing, or have never thought about that we might discover are what we love doing most of all.

So, just as discovering your Gifts is an iterative and evolving process, so is discovering your Passions. We don't know what we don't know, and until and unless we do, some of the elements of the sweet spot, the natural work we were meant to do, cannot be identified.

And although our intellect, which drives our Gifts, evolves rather slowly over our lives, our emotions, which underlie our Passions, can change quickly, as our bodies change and our experiences color what we care about.

Here are a few questions to ponder when thinking about what your Passion or Passions might be:

- In other people's observation, what do you seem to enjoy the most? What activities cause you to smile or sing while you do them? What is it about these activities that makes them so enjoyable?
- What have you done, or tried to do, that you really loathed? What made it so awful?
- What tasks do you take on with most relish, whether you are good at them or not? What do people get you to do because they know you will take it on enthusiastically?
- Intuitively, if someone asked you what your "ideal job" might be, how would you answer?
- If you've taken interest tests, where did they suggest your passions lie?
- What did you enjoy most in school, whether or not you were good at it?
- What hobbies or recreational activities that you do, or have done, do you or did you most enjoy? Why?
- What do you most enjoy working with: people, tools, ideas, or information?
- If you suddenly received a lot of money, or a lot of power, what would you do with it, and what would you start doing that you're not doing now, and why?

Here are some additional questions, posed by Neil Crofts in his book *Authentic Business*,[5] for helping you find your Passions:

- When do you feel at your most motivated?
- When do you get lost in activity or thought and lose all track of time?

- When do you feel alive, focused, and engaged?
- What is the common thread between smiling at the rain, enjoying the earth in your hands, putting on a sumptuous feast, and playing with your child?
- What is the focus of all your "flow" activities, the pivot around which they turn, the outcome to which they all drive?
- What is your nonnegotiable dream, so precious that so far you have told no one about it for fear it will be compromised?

Crofts believes in "following your passion," and that your Passions directly determine your Purpose. My experience has been that you're better off starting with unmet needs to discover your Purpose, but no one answer works for everyone. Crofts says you should write down your answers to the above questions, and discuss them with as many people as possible, starting with those you trust, until it is crafted into something that is not only your Passions but also your Purpose (the overlaps in Areas 3 and 4 of the three-circles chart). Then whenever anyone asks "What You Do?", you instead tell them your Purpose. And you build from there, using the principle of intentionality until the realization of this Purpose becomes your successful, "authentic" business, your Natural Enterprise.

What, you may ask, is the difference between something you have a Passion for and something you care deeply about? Once again, the difference is what's *natural*: Passions are emotional, instinctive, things you love doing without having to think about them or be persuaded that they're "the right thing to do." Things you care about can include causes that you have taken up because intellectually they seem worthy, or because someone you love has persuaded you that they are worth caring about, or out of a sense of duty.

We care about things we are passionate about, but we aren't always passionate about everything we care about. We don't love doing everything we do because we care about it. It's the things we naturally love doing that are our Passions.

A few years ago, Po Bronson wrote a book called *What Should I Do With My Life?*[26] that might be of use in identifying your Passions.

The book (and accompanying Web site) includes many stories about people who, at pivotal points in their lives, walked away from meaningless jobs and pursued, with varying degrees of success, their Passions.

An exercise I invented that some people have found useful for thinking about their Passions is what I call the Obit Exercise. It involves writing your obituary, focusing on accomplishments you hope to have achieved by the end of your life. If you try it, you'll probably find that these accomplishments will be around things you have true Passion for. (They also may give you some ideas for what you may subconsciously perceive your Gifts and Purposes to be.) If you want an example, try my Obit Exercise on my blog.[7]

You may think you know intuitively what your Passion or Passions are. Or you may have absolutely no idea. But it's time again to start homing in on the sweet spot, so turn to page 61 with the working copy of the three circles.

Thinking about the questions on the previous pages, or what your instincts tell you, write in the Passion circle some of the things you think your Passion or Passions might be, the things you love doing or are reasonably sure you would (if you had the time or opportunity) love doing.

Don't try to think ahead to the sweet spot: Your Gifts, your Passions, and your Purpose probably overlap somewhere, but at this point, I want you to focus *just* on your Passions, what you love doing. Don't discount them just because you have no Gift for them, or because you don't think there's a market for them. If they're your Passions, they're your Passions. In some respects, it's even more important to know what Passions you have that *don't* overlap your Gifts and your Purpose, because most of us will be tempted to work at what we're Gifted at, but long to do what we're Passionate about—a recipe for unhappiness and meaningless work.

Don't worry if you're not sure what to write. The journey is just starting, and we'll come back to this soon. Later in this chapter we'll describe some examples of Passions that various people have identified for themselves. And I'll tell you my own story and how I filled in and used the three circles to find my sweet spot.

Next step: Identifying your Purpose.

Your Purpose: What's needed that you care about

The third of the natural work circles is your Purpose. It starts with identifying human needs that are not currently met by the myriad of products and services that existing organizations are producing.

These must be needs that you care about. You may find or create an enterprise that taps perfectly into your Gifts and your Passions, but if it's producing something you don't care about, you will soon start to find that it becomes meaningless work. Two out of three isn't good enough, even though most of us spend our lives settling for two out of three, or less.

The absolute essence of effective entrepreneurship is research and innovation, and both are involved in discovering unmet needs. Chapters 3 and 4 of this book delve into these processes in detail, but if you don't know much about the processes of research and innovation, you might want to consider reading these chapters to know

> Your Purpose must be discovered, not invented. It starts with needs, not with solutions.

what you will have to do to really understand what the unmet needs in our society are and how Natural Enterprises succeed at meeting them.

At this stage, some intelligent guesses on unmet needs will suffice. Your Purpose is meeting those unmet needs you care about. In *Is Your Genius at Work?*,[8] Dick Richards elaborates:

- Your Purpose must be discovered, not invented. It starts with needs, not with solutions.
- Your Purpose is directed outward—it is the specific, tangible way in which your Gift is given to the world.
- Knowing your Purpose allows you to be more intentional and effective in fulfilling it.

- Your Purpose gives focus and meaning to your life and directs your decisions on what to do.

Here are a few questions to ponder when thinking about what your Purpose might be:

- What stirs you? What's going on in the world that makes you want to get involved?
- How do other people see your Purpose? In what context have they said, at certain points of your life, "if you care so much about this, why don't you do something about it?"
- What incidents in your life have suggested that what you thought you might be meant to do is not your Purpose after all?
- What have you had the courage to survive and overcome, and where did that courage come from?
- What "aha!" moments or "callings" have come to you in moments of reflection or crisis?
- What recurring ideals and intentions and unmet needs and possibilities have intrigued you for much of your life?
- What, most of all, do you think is needed in the world, in your country, your community, your profession, your current workplace?
- What do you feel responsible for, that you think you might be able to help improve?

You may think you know intuitively what your Purpose is. Or you may have absolutely no idea. But turn again to page 61 with the working copy of the three circles.

Thinking about the questions on the previous page, or what your instincts tell you, write in the blank Purpose circle some of the things you think your Purpose might be, the things you believe are needed, needs that are not met at all well by existing products and services, needs that you care about.

Don't try to think ahead to the sweet spot: Your Gift, your Passion, and your Purpose probably overlap somewhere, but at this point, I want you to focus *just* on your Purpose, what you believe there is an unmet need for, that you care about. Don't discount a Purpose just because you have no Gift for it, or because although you care about it, you'd dread actually doing it.

For example, a Purpose I care about a great deal is reducing animal cruelty. But although I've had the option of working at a local animal shelter, and doing firsthand research on factory farming, I just don't have the stomach for it. I would probably end up killing someone who had abused animals. This is the difference between caring for something—a cause—and having a Passion for work in that area, something you would love doing, or even do for free.

In some respects, it's even more important to know what Purposes you care about that *don't* overlap your Gifts and your Passions, because most of us will be drawn to work connected to those Purposes, but be both incompetent and unhappy doing it. We need to know this, so we can avoid trying to find work that is, perhaps, meaningful, but also dreadful and stifling.

Don't worry if you're not sure what to write. The journey is still just starting, and we'll come back to this soon.

You now have a first stab at what might be your Gifts, your Passions, and your Purposes. Don't worry about looking for overlaps yet. The next section will describe what some other people have thought to be their Gifts, Passions, and Purpose, and these may help you to home in on your own.

Some real-life examples of Gifts, Passions, and Purposes

My neighbor John tells a story I have heard from many people I know. He's caught in a job that pays quite well, but not well enough that he can quit and think about what he'd really like to do. He hates his job, and his health is suffering because of it.

His Gift is *figuring out how things work and how to make them work better.* (When you're as useless with machinery as I am, this is the kind of neighbor you want.) Even though he can afford to have an expert come in when something in his house breaks down, he prefers to do his own research and fix it himself, because he knows he'll do a better job (and if it breaks again, he'll know exactly how to fix it). He is the most mechanically inclined person I've ever met.

John's Passion, and his hobby, is *restoring old cars.* His house is full of vintage auto memorabilia, and he's always in the process of restoring, on weekends, at least two cars. When he's working on them, all the stress that normally shows in his face disappears. He'd like to race them, too, and he's a great driver.

John has never figured out what his Purpose is. He is self-sacrificing to a fault for his family, and clearly cares for them deeply. But he married young, and in the words of the Carly Simon song, I think he would say: "I never learned to be just me first, by myself."

As a result, finding his Purpose will be a challenge. But probably less of a challenge than finding his Gift and Passion might be, if they weren't so clear in his mind. At this point in his life, he doesn't think he wants to be, or could be, an entrepreneur. His priorities are his family and looking after the bills.

Any of three things could change that. He might get so fed up with his meaningless work that, despite the extra stress it would impose on him, he would quit. The company he works for might fold. Or his Purpose might suddenly come to him, as a result of some unpredictable event touching him personally, and if it overlaps his Gift and Passion, he will suddenly get the courage to pursue it, working with or for others, or creating his own enterprise, working naturally.

My friend Howard, like many people, has always followed his Gift rather than his Passion. He has a knack for numbers and has parlayed that into a comfortable, easy career. His Gift is *finding ways to use software more effectively.* Financial software, search software, problem-solving software, you name it, Howard will show you how to save time and improve productivity with it. More generally, his Gift is *making more with less.*

His Passions are *sculpting* and *tackling intractable problems.* He's pursued the former as a hobby (and he's really good at it, but not, he suspects, enough to make a living at it). He's looking to get more into the latter in his next career.

His Purpose is *to cure diseases.* He discovered it after already choosing (and succeeding in) a career in financial services.

He just recently started working for the local health department, helping with emergency preparedness for infectious diseases and developing software for disease surveillance and emergency communication. He's getting close to the sweet spot, and looking to get even closer.

My young colleague Karen has a more difficult challenge. Her Gift is *inspiring people*—she's exuberant, galvanizing, even charismatic. If she wanted to, she could get people to walk on coals.

But she doesn't want to. Her passion is *pattern-seeking*, and she works in a job that lets her do this, since part of it entails collecting, analyzing, and interpreting large amounts of data. She describes herself as a geek, and can get engrossed in computer charts and statistical analyses for hours.

The paradox is that, since she is such a natural leader, she has already been promoted to roles that involve more people management and less data analysis, so she's getting restless. *What do you do when your Gifts and your Passions don't overlap at all?*

My guess is that, as she starts to discover her Purpose, this disconnect will resolve itself. Like many people, she's had a challenging life, and had to cope with a lot of personal and family challenges that have prevented her from learning about and focusing on longer-term life goals and objectives.

Paul is about the same age as Karen. He's had a relatively easy life, and is absolutely driven to make a difference in the world. His Gift is *activating people*—some might even say provoking them. You can't talk with him for five minutes without wanting to rush out and do something in response to information he's given you or some concern he's expressed. He speaks calmly but passionately and persuasively.

His Passion is *communicating new information.* Naturally enough, he is a blogger, but he's as passionate about speaking as about writing, and he realizes it is more immediate and compelling. He loves first-hand research (interviewing and observing) and digging out what no one else has discovered.

His Purpose is *bringing about large-scale social change.* It's pretty easy to see the sweet spot for him as being either journalism or politics. But Paul realizes how ineffective both of these have been in achieving his Purpose. My guess is that he will become an entrepreneur, working with a progressive social service or health service organization for which he'll be the spokesman and/or lead researcher.

Now, after hearing about my neighbors, you may be curious to know my own Gifts, Passions, and Purpose. Here is my chart:

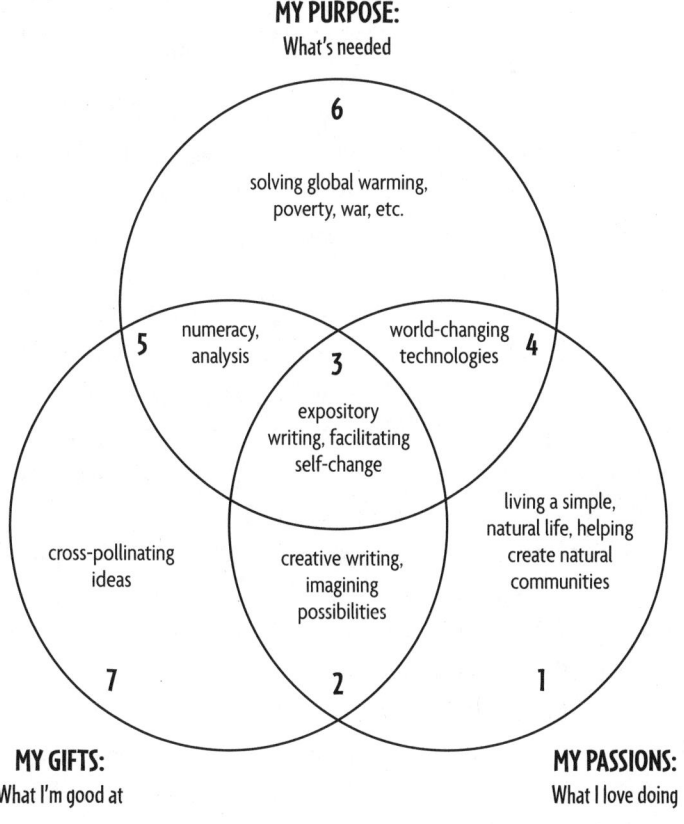

My Gifts are:

- Cross-pollinating ideas: Applying knowledge learned from one domain to very different domains. I've had this ability all my life. I can be reading an esoteric scientific journal and be able to see how some new discovery applies in a business, social, educational, or health context.
- Creative and expository writing.
- Imagining possibilities: When a challenge arises, or as a creative exercise, thinking about what might be possible approaches, ideas, visions.
- Facilitating self-change, in myself and in others: Making it easier for people to think differently, change their ideas and behaviors, and creating and giving them the tools to do so, to become who they really are.

For a long time, I thought the first of these Gifts, the ability to cross-pollinate ideas, might be my sweet spot. I finally realized that, although I am good at this, it is less valued than I thought it would be (traditional businesses that can afford to pay for innovative people don't tend to value innovation very highly), and it is not something I am Passionate about. I was frustrated trying to market this talent.

Much of my life I spent working at financial services jobs I was reasonably competent at, and that there was a market for (thanks to government audit, accounting, securities, and tax regulations). These were successful but disengaging jobs in Area 5 of the natural work circles—I had no Passion for them and they were, for me, meaningless, often parasitic jobs.

I would love to be able to invent technologies that might make life better, such as foods made from vegetable sources that had the flavor, texture, and nutritional value of meats (so we could rid the world of factory farms), or simpler, more effective, less invasive long-term birth-control technologies. The world needs these things, and I have a Passion for them, but, alas, no Gift, so, for me, they are Area 4 activities, not in my sweet spot.

And although I have a personal Passion for living a radically simple lifestyle, this is an Area 1 Passion: I am not particularly good at it, and the world, at least so far, doesn't have an appetite for it. I also have a Passion for interspecies communication, because if we could learn their languages, I think many animals and birds have an enormous amount to teach us. But the world isn't ready to invest in this, and I have no special Gift for this kind of work anyway, so it's on my Area 1 list.

There is no question that there is a need to come to grips with the intractable problems facing our society: global warming, poverty, war, and so on. These problems are beyond *my* competence to solve and I am increasingly dubious that they are within anyone's competence to solve. I have watched with great interest George Monbiot's book *Heat*[9] and campaign to address global warming through a series of radical global changes that would reduce greenhouse gases by 90 percent by 2030. Despite the support of Al Gore, hundreds of climate scientists, and other people with great Gifts and Passions in this area, I am not optimistic that they will succeed. I hope I am wrong, and if I am, I might well be reengaged to play my part in this effort. I am not holding my breath. These, for me, are Area 6 activities.

Although I continue to have both a Gift and a Passion for creative writing, and for imagining possibilities, I share these Gifts and Passions with many other people, and the market for our offerings is much smaller than the supply. These will likely remain just hobbies for me, Area 2 activities.

That leaves just two candidates for the sweet spot, the Area 3 where my Gift and Passion meet an important, unmet human need:

- Expository writing: The publication of this book, and the success of my blog and other written work, indicate that this Gift and Passion is in my sweet spot, and
- Facilitating self-change: My blog, *How to Save the World*, offers my personal thoughts and experience to help people understand how the world really works, and how to cope with it and make it better in small, important ways. Its continuing

success, measured by comments from readers, and the successes I have had helping people do their work more effectively in my employment and work contracts, suggests that this Gift and Passion are also in my sweet spot. I want to help people find natural work, and to create Natural Enterprises, and I have some useful lessons to pass on about what works and what doesn't, in the process of helping people understand, adapt, and change themselves, naturally.

My chart would have looked much different a few years ago, and I suspect that in the future it will continue to evolve as the market, my interests, and my self-knowledge change.

I'm writing this in December, 2007. During the summer of 2007 I became the Vice President of the Canadian Institute of Chartered Accountants (the Canadian counterpart of the American Institute for Certified Professional Accountants). My role is to help our coworkers, our 83,000 members, and the million-plus entrepreneurial businesses in Canada to succeed.

I wasn't looking for the position, although I had been talking with the CICA about sponsoring an entrepreneurial Center of Excellence, which would let entrepreneurs learn from and help each other (with my facilitation), and conduct research on (and perhaps teach) the skills entrepreneurs need to succeed.

When I was approached about the VP position, instead of studying what the CICA did, I told them my vision for what the CICA could do to transform the Canadian economy from a fragile, resource- and export-dependent economy to a resilient and innovative economy by helping the CICA's members (accountants and consultants) to learn to help entrepreneurs, as I had done with my quarterly breakfasts.

They liked the vision, and gave me the job of realizing it. Finally, a chance to apply my Gift and Passion to my Purpose, within an *existing* organization, and to help other Natural Entrepreneurs find their sweet spots and found enterprises that fulfill them.

But I know that beyond that, I am destined to create a Natural Enterprise with others with complementary Gifts and Passions and a shared Purpose of "facilitating self-change." I'm thinking this through even now on my blog,[10] and you're welcome to join that conversation!

Here are some more thoughts and ideas on how to identify the sweet spot where your Gifts, Passions, and Purpose intersect.

Following your Passion versus asking "Who needs your Gifts now?"

Although we each need to find or create the work where our Gifts (what we do uniquely well), our Passions (what we love doing), and our Purpose (what is needed that we care about) intersect, it's hard to know where to start. Many self-help books recommend that you "follow your Passion," so this might seem to be the most logical place to start.

But here's another idea: Rather than starting by searching for or creating that perfect enterprise that fulfills our Passions the way the ones we are doing now can never hope to do, perhaps we should instead set ourselves the simpler task of asking the question *Who Needs Our Gifts Now?* and then follow where the answer to that question takes us.

This approach essentially starts with identifying your Purpose (what is needed that you care about) and looking for overlaps between it and your Gifts. The results will be in either Area 3 or Area 5 of the three-circles chart.

By asking the question this way, with the emphasis on urgent, even desperate human needs (rather than just "wants"), you are more likely, I think, to find that you have some Passion for the ideas you come up with—so these ideas are more likely to be in Area 3 (the sweet spot) than Area 5.

The caution here is that, although you may care very much about such desperate needs, and may have a Gift that can address them, your Passion must be genuine and unforced. We may want to end world poverty, but the idea of facing people who are enduring immense misery and suffering every day may be unbearable to us.

It is not natural work if we don't love doing it every day, even though it may be meaningful. This is an important distinction. If you can answer the question *Who Needs Your Gifts Now?* but the idea of doing work fulfilling those needs fills you with dread, this is Area 5 work. Keep looking for the sweet spot.

Settling for too little: Work that you thought was in the sweet spot but isn't

In my discussions with work colleagues, friends, and customers past and present, I've concluded that most of us spend most of our work lives doing work that is either in Area 2 (unneeded work we're good at and love) or Area 5 (marketable work that we're good at but don't love).

I call these two intersections, respectively, *unappreciated* and *disengaged* work. They are both seductive, albeit for different reasons.

Many independent consultants, including a bumper crop of Baby Boomers who have been outsourced, downsized, or just squeezed out as a cost-cutting measure by their employers, end up selling their services as sole proprietors, doing what they used to do before they were let go.

They get into a cycle of addiction to these jobs. Because they were released involuntarily, they are often down on themselves, so when the market for their services turns out to be very difficult, they think that's their fault—they're just not selling themselves or marketing their services well.

So they work harder, longer, for less money. Whatever Passion they may have had for this work disappears, so they feel not only unappreciated but also frustrated. But they are like Lucky, the dog whose story I told in the introduction: This work is the only life they know. They cannot imagine doing other work. They don't have the self-confidence to try something different, or to look for partners with complementary Gifts and Passions who could shift their work from Areas 2 or 5 to the Area 3 sweet spot (more on this in Chapter 2).

It is even possible that the work they are doing *used to be* appreciated, and met an important unmet need, but because of changing market conditions or disruptive innovations by others (see Chapter 4), this work has slid from Area 3 to Area 2 and perhaps even to Area

1. But because it used to be sweet-spot work, they won't let go of it. They are like the people who keep trying to rekindle a relationship that has died long ago.

Before you conclude that working for yourself, doing what you do now for someone else, is what you're looking for, make sure it meets an important need that is unmet by others (including your old employer!), and that it is something you really love, not just something you are comfortable with. Don't let a lack of self-confidence, or a lack of knowledge of what's possible and what's needed, lock you into Area 2 work.

The challenge with disengaged, Area 5 work is just as great, and it is just as easy to get addicted to it. This is work that is appreciated, easy for you (because you have a Gift for it), and possibly quite well paid. You might even blame yourself for not having a Passion for it (or losing your Passion for it), and feel that all you need is some time off to rekindle that Passion.

You know better, though. There is a reason you no longer love doing this work.

You may think this is the work environment, the boss, or the people you work with. You may quit, for reasons not all that different from the people who leave because they are unappreciated, and go into competition with your old employer, either in your own company (most likely with yourself as the only employee, because you don't want the hassle of dealing with other staff or partners), or working with a competitor of your old employer.

I know a lot of people who have done this. Most of them have jumped from the frying pan into the fire. And it's not because their ex-employer sued them for violating noncompete clauses in their employment agreement—such clauses are surprisingly rarely enforced.

It's because it was the work, not the workplace, most of them had lost Passion for, and doing the same work in another workplace changed nothing. Worse, because they had to rebuild their customer base and reputation, the work became much harder than the old work, so the fact that it was easy—one of the factors that kept them in it so long—no longer applied. It went from being Area 5 work to Area 6 work—even farther from the sweet spot.

The lesson here is not to settle for too little. The work you were meant to do, natural work, is out there. You may have to do a lot of research, and a lot of self-discovery, to find it. But it's worth it—life is too short (or perhaps too long) to spend most of it doing work that is tedious, stressful, meaningless, and unnatural.

Don't forget your hobbies

The things you do for recreation are probably Area 1 activities—things you do just because you love them, because you have a Passion for them. But some of them also may fulfill an important unmet need—and be part of your Purpose. And some may be things you have a Gift for. For now, just put them in the Passion circle on your copy of the three-circles chart.

The challenge of not knowing what we don't know

Most of us struggle to try to "move" work that is currently in Area 5 (stuff we're good at, and that has a market, but that doesn't fulfill us) to Area 3. Or we try to "create" a market, through promotion, for work we love and are good at, and hence move a thankless and unprofitable business (Area 2) to Area 3. I have argued that both of these efforts are somewhat futile, and that the work in the "sweet spot" (Area 3) exists (for each of us) and needs to be *discovered* rather than manufactured.

Most of us, though, simply don't know enough to know how to discover it, or even how to go about beginning to discover it.

There is no silver-bullet approach to this discovery process. You can try starting with who you want to work with, and then work with them to discover work that is needed, which the collective group is good at, and which each member of the group can work within, doing work that they love.

Or you can try asking the question *Who needs your Gifts now?* And in Chapter 3 I'll suggest a way to learn more about what's needed. For those who have a pretty good understanding of what's needed (goods and services that are *recognized* as needed and *affordable* by those who need it), but are not at all excited about making a living filling that need, I have no suggestion other than *keep looking.*

What helped me most was looking first for the Gift/Passion overlap. To find this overlap, I considered each item in my Gift and Passion lists in turn and asked:

- What kinds of things might I best be doing that draw on this Gift and Passion? and
- Do I really *want* to do those things more than anything else?

So I started by asking myself what kinds of work would give expression to each of my Gifts. And then I asked myself if I would genuinely enjoy spending a large part of my time and energy doing such work. This enabled me to whittle down the list of overlap candidates quickly. Because (I think) I have a pretty good imagination, this might be easier for me than for others, however.

I also found that deciding on my Purpose also focused my understanding of my Passions. Finding that sweet spot in Area 3 really requires approaching it from all three circles, using a large amount of imagination, iteration, soul-searching, and exploring and researching each possibility until you find one that intersects all three. Several times I've thought I'd found some Area 3 opportunities, only to find, on further consideration and research, that I'd overestimated the market or my interest or skill in doing them.

It also can be useful to explore the Area 4 opportunities more closely—perhaps by partnering with others who have skills you lack, together you might be able to make a living, each doing what you love, using your Gifts and Passions, producing a *collective* product that is needed. Trying to make a living alone makes the task unnecessarily difficult. I'll talk about that more in Chapter 2.

Two things often will prevent us, or at least delay us, from finding those intersections. The first is

> Two things often will prevent us from finding our intersections. The first is unawareness of markets and opportunities. Not knowing enough about ourselves is the second blocker.

unawareness of markets and opportunities—not knowing what is needed, by whom. This is doubly difficult because quite often the people who have a need that we could fill don't realize they have it.

We may need to imagine it, bring it to the surface, explore it with those who may need it, codevelop the solution to that need with them. And if they still don't recognize that they need it, then they don't need it yet, and we are too far ahead.

Not knowing enough about ourselves is the second blocker. If our work and life experience is limited or unvaried, we may not really know what our Gifts, or even our Passions, are, and can't be expected to until we have broadened our experience.

Volunteering, travel, research, and exchange programs can speed up this process, but to some extent we have to give ourselves time for our Gifts and our Passions to emerge.

Five questions to ask if you're stuck

If you're struggling to come up with what to write in one or more of the three circles on the natural work chart, here are five more questions to ask yourself that might help:

> **What do you see yourself doing when you retire?** Is there a way you could make a living doing something like this now? If it's traveling, could you make a living as a maker of travelogues, as a travel-guide writer, or as a guide or in some facet of the hospitality industry? If it's spending time in nature, could you find a job teaching others why you love it? If it's watching sports, could you make a living as a commentator or analyst?
>
> **What are you doing to explore what's possible?** Most of us kind of drift into traditional jobs because we're convinced that's all there is, or because it's the path of least resistance. We have no idea what's possible, how some people actually are making a living doing things we would love to do. The Internet is full of information. There are books like Po Bronson's *What Should I Do With My Life?* that tell inspiring stories of people who have discovered their Passions and applied it to their Purpose,

and how they did it. And through social networking, you can find and talk with people who are doing what you've always wanted to do.

What are you doing to become better at what you love? Is the fact that you're not skilled or knowledgeable about something you always secretly wanted to do just a convenient excuse for not overcoming the fear of trying to be good at it? If courage is merely not having any alternative but to do something remarkable, what can you do to make trying to become expert at something you think you'd really love so compelling you have no alternative but to go for it?

Have you considered trying something out? This could be on a volunteer or short-term basis that will show you whether or not it's your Passion or your Purpose without the need to make a long-term commitment to it.

Have you tried the "two-job option"? If you're really convinced that your Gifts, Passions, and Purpose are irreconcilable, have you considered what Paul Graham[11] calls the "two-job option": work at things you don't love (Area 5 work) to get money to work on things you do (Area 1 and 2 work)?

One final suggestion: Do this exercise of listing your Gifts, Passions, and Purpose with others—people you love, people who know you, people who are on the same journey, even people you might want to make a living with. The more information you can bring to bear, the more likely you are to develop an accurate list, and the more likely the sweet spot is to emerge.

Seeking the sweet spot as a lifelong journey

Over our lifetimes, our Gifts, our Passions, and what is needed change. So inevitably the sweet spot where they intersect will change and evolve. Furthermore, as you learn more about what is needed, and about yourself, you will be able to assess your sweet spot more accurately.

Last year I was diagnosed as having ulcerative colitis, a chronic disease that is triggered and exacerbated by stress. At that point, one of the first things I did was to give up my innovation consulting practice, which initially I had hoped would be in the sweet spot but which turned out to be in Area 2 (unappreciated)—and produced far more stress than was good for me.

I initially had thought that in order to find stress-free work, I would have to settle for (another) Area 5 job—something I'm good at, and in high demand, but probably something I wouldn't be passionate about.

But then I realized I was thinking about it all wrong. If my Gifts and my Passions were shifting (from really ambitious, exciting work to more modest, local, fun work), the answer wasn't to give up on finding the sweet spot, but rather to

- redefine the type of work I was searching for,
- research and assess the need for that kind of work, and
- find work partners, people to make a living with, whose Gifts and Passions are complementary to my own and who, in partnership with me, could allow us all to fulfill our purposes while collectively meeting a currently unmet need.

One of the areas where my Gifts and Passions overlap is *imagining possibilities*—coming up with novel, creative answers to challenging problems, answers that no one else has, or would be likely to, come up with.

I also have some Gifts that I am not particularly passionate about (research, analysis, intelligence-gathering, and applying my experience, learning, and other people's stories to solve business problems). And I have some Passions that I am not particularly gifted in (creating sustainable, intentional communities and developing radically simple sustainable-living programs).

For me, natural work *might* include using those Gifts I am not particularly Passionate about (provided that isn't *all* it includes) and ideally would allow me to learn about, develop, and try out some of the Passions that I am not currently very Gifted in.

So, for example, my business partners might be very good at creating sustainable, intentional communities, and that might be part of our collective Natural Enterprise's mandate, offering me the opportunity to participate in this type of activity without getting in over my head.

My Purpose (what I'm meant to do) used to be *provoking change.* Recently my thinking on this has been shifting as well, as a result of my growing awareness of the enormous difficulty of bringing about change in complex systems. My Purpose now has become the humbler *facilitating self-change,* enabling people individually and in groups to learn more about and understand how to allow themselves (individually and collectively in groups) to adapt to and accommodate ever-changing social and environmental conditions.

You, too, are likely to find that your Gifts, Passions, and Purpose will evolve over time.

Finding the sweet spot all comes down to the iterative, complex challenge of finding the ideal partners for your enterprise—those whose skills and interests complement your own, and who allow each partner to exercise his/her Gifts and Passions and fulfill his/her Purpose while *collectively* meeting a currently unmet need. In my experience, sole proprietorship, trying to do everything in your enterprise yourself, is not the way to go—it is unnecessarily tedious, risky, exhausting, and stressful. Much better to share the load with people you love to work with. In Chapter 2, we will delve deeper into the three-circles chart and find the sweet spot for the *collective* enterprise.

> In my experience, sole proprietorship, trying to do everything in your enterprise yourself, is unnecessarily tedious, risky, exhausting, and stressful.

So don't be in a hurry to look for intersections, or to find your sweet spot. If you think some of your Gifts or Passions are reciprocal, or that some of your Gifts or Passions are aligned with some important need that you care about, by all means pencil them in in the appropriate intersection of the three-circles chart. As you work through this book and learn what natural work you were meant to do, it will all become clearer. *What's truly in your sweet spot may not yet be on your chart at all.* You can't "move" a Gifts or Passions or Purpose into the sweet spot. It has to be discovered, allowed to emerge as you learn. Take your time.

You are welcome to post your three-circles work chart to the Finding Natural Partners Web site http://NaturalEnterprise.org/partners/, and share with others your Gifts, Passions, and Purpose, and start to explore how they might dovetail with others' in Natural Enterprise. As it evolves, it can be a record of your journey to find natural work, what you were meant to do.

Now we're going to look at the process of finding partners whose Gifts and Passions complement your own and who share your Purpose.

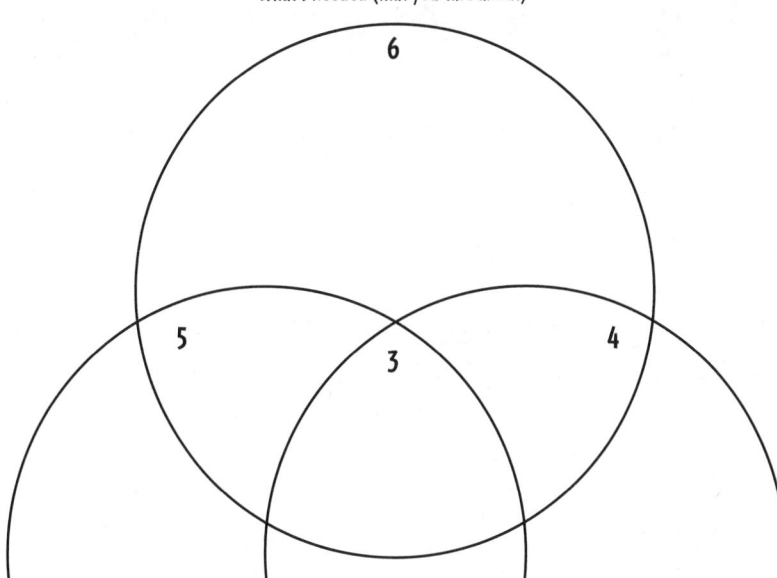

YOUR PURPOSE:
What's needed (that you care about)

YOUR GIFTS:
What you're uniquely good at

YOUR PASSIONS:
What you love doing

Area:
1. Self-indulgent
2. Unappreciated
3. *Fulfilled*
4. Disappointed
5. Disengaged
6. Self-sacrificing
7. Frustrated

FINDING THE RIGHT PARTNERS

discovering people whose skills complement your own

Seeking a shared Purpose

In Chapter 1, I showed a way to find the sweet spot where your Gift, your Passion, and your Purpose intersect. Now, I'm going to explain the process for aligning the intersection of your Gift, Passion, and Purpose with those of others—your prospective partners.

This is a four-step process:

1. First, you must find people who share your Purpose, or whose Purpose can be readily combined with yours to create a collective Purpose you can all embrace.
2. Next, you must ensure that your Gifts (the ones that overlap your Passions and your Purpose), and those of the people you have found who share your Purpose, are:
   a. Mutually Exclusive: not significantly overlapping (otherwise you're likely to be stepping on each other's toes), *and*
   b. Collectively Sufficient to be able to achieve your Purpose, without "skill gaps" you would have to get outsiders to do, or do badly or indifferently.
3. Then, you need to make sure that, between you and your potential partners, you have all twelve core capacities prerequisite to any business' success, as outlined in the Introduction on pages 18–21.
4. And finally, you need to come to terms with your partners on what the Vision and Operating Principles of the enterprise will be, and what each of you needs to get from the enterprise to succeed, on your own terms, individually and collectively.

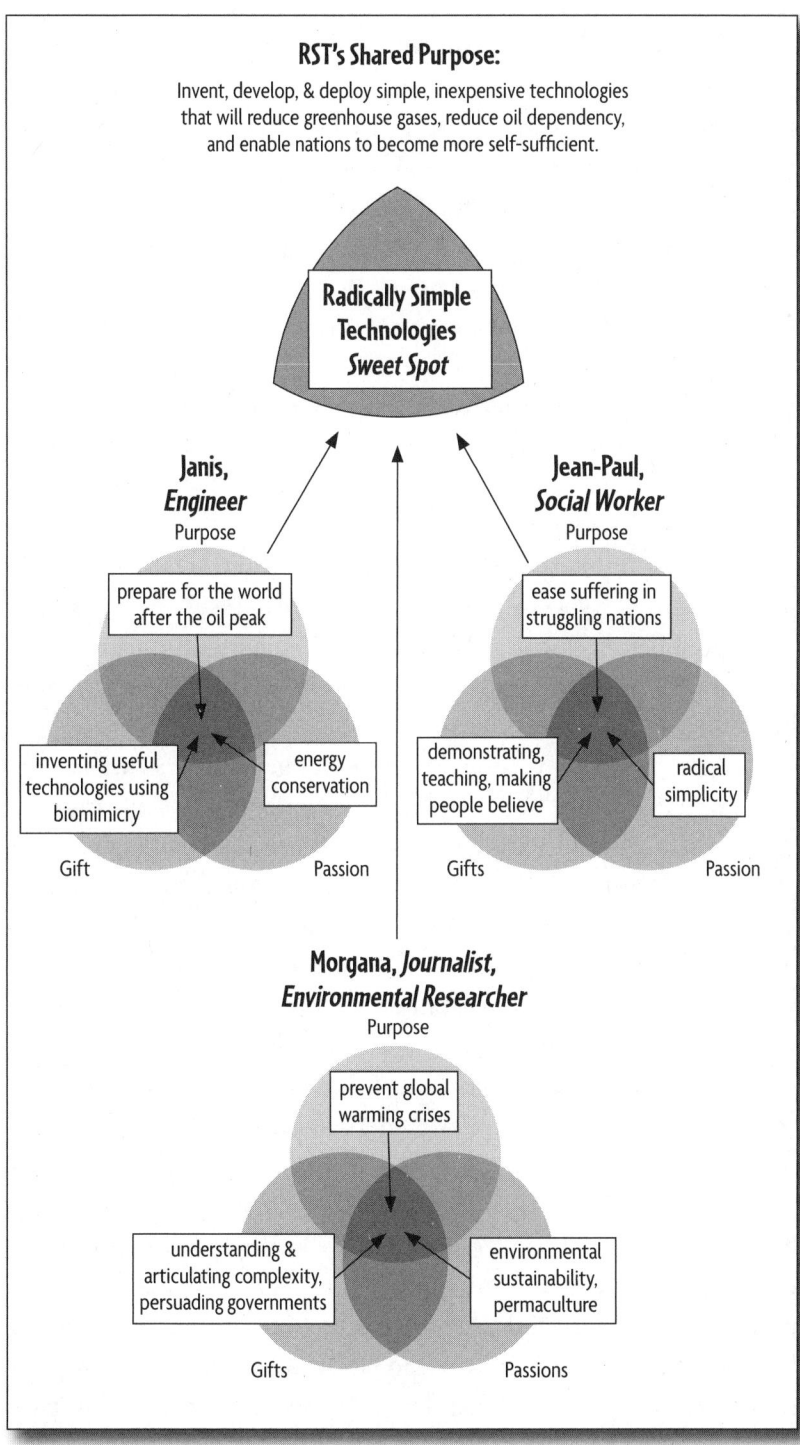

Let's look at an example to explain how this might work. Recall the three prospective entrepreneurs we met in the introduction, Janis, Morgana, and Jean-Paul (page 5). Let's look at what their Gifts, Passions, and Purposes might be, and how they might come to work together as partners in a Natural Enterprise.

Janis, our underemployed mid-career engineer, has defined one of her Gifts as *inventing useful technologies using biomimicry*, copying ideas from nature (the concept of biomimicry is explained in more detail in Chapter 3). One of her Passions is *energy conservation*. And her Purpose, inspired by James Kunstler's book *The Long Emergency*,[1] is to *prepare for the world after the oil peak*, when supplies of conventional hydrocarbons have begun to run out.

Although she has other Gifts and Passions, the ones noted above are the ones she believes intersect with her Purpose. She has long had a dream of working for a company that recognized her Gift and shared her Passion and Purpose, but she has found most energy companies are not interested in innovation unless it allows them to sell more nonrenewable energy.

Morgana, our not-yet-employed, newly graduated journalist and environmental researcher, has worked for a nonprofit foundation for the past year, aligned with her Passion for *environmental sustainability* and employing her Gifts for *understanding and articulating complexity* and *persuading governments* and others through her compelling writing and speaking ability. But her real Purpose, inspired by a meeting with Al Gore, the Purpose that intersects these Gifts and this Passion, is *preventing global warming crises.* The work she is doing currently is, she feels, preaching to the converted, and not getting anywhere.

Jean-Paul, our Baby Boomer, second-career-seeking social worker, has spent the past two years in Africa working with AIDS victims. His Gifts include *demonstrating* (showing people how to do things better), *teaching,* and *making people believe* through stories and critical argument. His Passions include living a life of "radical simplicity," inspired by Jim Merkel's book of the same name[2]—owning less, buying less, owing less. His Purpose is to *ease suffering in struggling nations.* He's been doing that, but he's frustrated at the slow pace of change, how few people he can help, and how little he can help them. He wants to do more.

The three of them meet, serendipitously, at an Open Space[3] event on the subject of Finding Imaginative Solutions to Intractable Problems. One of the sessions is on Inventing Simple, Inexpensive Technologies, and the three of them sign up for it. Janis talks about some of the inventions she's been working on—solar-powered light fixtures and water pumps, and an ingenious "hybrid" lightbulb that fits in regular light fixtures, and captures and runs on solar energy, but can be switched to run on electricity when its solar cell runs low—and Morgana and Jean-Paul are entranced.

During the next few days, the three meet again, and they develop a shared Purpose for an enterprise they tentatively call Radically Simple Technologies:

> to invent, develop, and deploy simple, inexpensive technolo-
> gies that will reduce greenhouse gases, reduce oil depen-
> dency, and enable nations to become more self-sufficient.

This Purpose embraces Janis's, Morgana's, and Jean-Paul's individual Purposes without diluting or contorting them. The fact that it was so easy to develop reflects the fact that they instinctively felt, when they first met, that they were meant to make a living together.

That's step 1.

Then they have to assess the mutual exclusivity and collective sufficiency of their Gifts. It's pretty clear that their Gifts are mutually exclusive: They aren't going to be battling over who does what.

That's step 2.

Their collective sufficiency is another matter. The process of establishing what additional Gifts they need will evolve as they determine what needs they are going to fill, and how, but they probably can make an intelligent guess at them now, and start looking for people who have those Gifts, are Passionate about them, and share the Purpose that Janis, Morgana, and Jean-Paul have identified.

The result of these two steps is shown in the diagram above.

Step 3 is to determine which of the partners have the twelve core capacities that any Natural Enterprise needs:

- Excellent business instincts
- Critical-thinking skills
- Imaginative skills
- Creative skills
- Attention skills
- Communication skills
- Demonstration skills
- Learning skills
- Responsibility
- Self-management skills
- Passion
- Collaboration skills

Ideally, more than one partner should have each of these capacities—mutual exclusivity is not an issue here. What is essential is that, among them, the partners of Radically Simple Technologies have all twelve capacities covered.

Step 4 is to assess:

- what shared Vision the partners have for the enterprise and the Operating Principles that fall out of that shared Vision, and
- what each of the partners needs and wants from the enterprise, to make sure they have a collective understanding of what commitment each partner is offering, what each is demanding in return, and therefore what the enterprise will have to achieve to meet those demands.

Janis, Morgana, and Jean-Paul, as they talk about how they imagine Radical Simple Technologies (RST) working, expand on their shared Purpose to create a shared Vision[4] for the enterprise—a portrait of how they see the enterprise operating a few years into the future.

This Vision *imagines what's possible.* Unlike most corporate "vision statements" that describe high-level objectives and measures the corporation is planning to achieve ("be the preeminent producer of . . ."), the collective Vision of prospective partners in Natural Enterprise tells a story about how they imagine operating, what they envision doing, and how, and to what end, and with what results. It's like the script of their future working lives, cowritten.

This Vision embodies the Operating Principles for the enterprise. Janis, Morgana, and Jean-Paul, as they articulate their vision, settle on the following Principles stemming from their shared values and the egalitarian, responsible approach they all want their Natural Enterprise to incorporate:

No managers, no hierarchy, no titles: Everyone manages themselves, and collectively manages the organization.

Only long-term, qualitative measures: Focus on the long-term well-being of the partners, customers, and community, not on short-term financial results.

Commitment to service: Partners are in the business to serve others, not to maximize their self-interest. The freedom of equal partnership brings with it responsibility for service and full engagement.

No secrecy: Complete information and the complete truth, all the time. That includes training everyone to understand the whole business ("business literacy") so they can make meaning of this information.

Compensation based on need, not performance: No individual ratings or rankings. Compensation is based on what the partners need, not on their impossible-to-determine "individual" performance. The principle here is that if you have kids and a mortgage, you need more compensation than the sixty-year-old with no debts; the traditional compensation model gets it exactly backward.

Decision-making by unanimous consensus and by empowerment of individual partners: All significant decisions, including decisions on acceptance of new partners and expulsion of partners, are made by unanimous consensus. Minor, day-to-day decisions are entrusted to the individual partners.

Sustainability and size limit: If the partnership, in the opinion of its partners, becomes unwieldy, it will split into two or more logical, networked organizations. This principle is intended to ensure the enterprise thrives without the need to grow, and is resilient as economic, social, and customer needs change.

Buy local: The enterprise as much as possible attempts to do business with other local organizations sharing its values in preference to purely profit-motivated and nonlocally owned enterprises.

High social and environmental responsibility: The enterprise maintains high social standards, including respect for others' rights, freedoms, and opinions; protection of the health and safety of partners, customers, and the community; contribution to the welfare of the society beyond just the enterprise's partners; and high environmental standards, including minimization of waste and pollution, optimizing use of renewable resources, sustainability without the need to grow and consume more resources over time, using cradle-to-cradle production and distribution processes, and having a small ecological footprint.

Work isn't everything: The enterprise recognizes that there is more to life than work, and strives to allow partners as much time to pursue other activities as possible without critically compromising the enterprise's ability to achieve well-being for its partners.

No absentee ownership: All enterprise partners must live in the community and be active in the enterprise. All assets are shared by all partners communally. The enterprise does not incur liabilities except in extraordinary circumstances, when these debts are repaid in full within a year, and only when the creditors are partners.

Responsibility to partners, customers, and community: Enterprise partners agree to accept collective responsibility for the well-being of all partners, customers, and those in the communities in which it operates.

The temptation to settle for less

Whether you're looking to find a Natural Enterprise or to create your own, the process for finding the right partners outlined above is an onerous one. All kinds of things can go wrong. If you're looking to create a Natural Enterprise:

- You may not be able to find anyone who shares your Purpose.
- You may find that most of the people who share your Purpose also share your Gifts—you all have the same skills (so you'll be falling all over each other if you try to work together).
- The people you share a Purpose with may lack many of the essential Gifts the enterprise needs, so you may be tempted to hire or subcontract them.
- The people you share a Purpose with may lack many of the twelve critical capacities a Natural Enterprise needs, so you may be tempted to hire or subcontract them.
- Despite your shared Purpose, you may not be able to agree on a shared Vision or Operating Principles.

If your current work is bad enough, or if you're unemployed and desperate enough, you may be tempted to settle for less, and to try to create a Natural Enterprise that just doesn't meet the criteria, or to look for another meaningless job.

But in the most joyful, responsible, sustainable, truly Natural Enterprises I know, the partners didn't settle for less. Perhaps they were lucky that they didn't have to.

The last thing you want to do is put all this thought, energy, and effort into finding Natural Work and then find yourself in another job you dread. The world is filled with entrepreneurs who hoped for the best and now dread getting up in the morning and facing a job, the job that they created for themselves, that they hate.

> The last thing you want to do is put all this thought, energy, and effort into finding Natural Work and then find yourself in another job you dread.

A Natural Enterprise is a partnership. In that respect, it's a lot like a marriage. There are some marriages that work out brilliantly because of sheer dumb luck. But many marriages fail because the partners lack or lose a shared purpose (e.g., when their children are grown and move away), or because the strengths and weaknesses they bring to the relationship are mismatched (and the marriage counselor is unable to help them bridge the critical "skill gap" that's keeping them from getting along). Or because the needs of one partner or another just aren't being met, and can't be. Or because their visions for the future are incompatible. Or because the principles by which they live their lives are irreconcilable.

> **A Natural Enterprise is a partnership. In that respect, it's a lot like a marriage.**

Just like Natural Enterprises.

And although instinct and chemistry are valuable in both types of partnerships, we tend to depend heavily on these "irrational" factors when we decide whether or not to marry. In a business partnership, it is wise to temper that instinctive, chemical attraction for others with more sober and systematic evaluation.

By all means, trust your instincts, and if your heart tells you that the people you have just discovered are the people you were meant to make a living with, pay attention.

But be careful you don't settle too quickly or rely solely on emotions in your desire to find work that seems, perhaps, to be at least *more* natural, more meaningful, than the dreadful work you are doing today, or in your desire to end the anxiety of unemployment or unsuccessful entrepreneurship.

Just as the person you were *really* meant to love and live with is out there, somewhere, waiting to be discovered, so too is the enterprise you were meant to make a living at, naturally, joyfully, waiting to be created.

How and where to look for partners

So how do you find the people with whom you were meant to make a living?

I wish there were an easy answer. The short answer is to meet with and talk with a lot of people, based on what you've learned about them and who others have recommended you speak with.

I recently wrote an article on my blog that ended with a question for my readers:

> Why is it that, despite the relatively low survival rate of sole proprietorships, most people who decide to start their own business do it alone?

Ed, one of my blog's wise readers, responded:

> I think the following are the reasons why people go into business alone:
> 1. It is hard to find someone you know well enough that you know you can partner with them through the good and the bad.
> 2. It is harder to find such a person with the right set of skills to complement yours.
> 3. It is yet harder to find such a person who has the same entrepreneurial spirit as you do.
>
> Lately I've been thinking about how I could put together a team of people to work together and create products that will add value to other people's lives and put money in our pockets without having to work for a corporation and create value for that corporation while we don't get to benefit from what we create. . . .
>
> I am thinking about going back to school (grad school), finding people with similar interests, developing face-to-face relationships and going from there. . . . I often hear

people working together across the globe through blogs, wikis, e-mail, and IM and I admire it. I don't know how they find each other and make it work.

Not so different from the reasons some people never get married (or having failed at marriage, never try it again), is it?

Although the right approach to finding partners with whom to make a living depends on your personality and your situation, here are a couple of approaches that might work for you.

The search for partners need not (indeed, it must not) involve compromising your values or what you want to do. It should enable you to do what you do best, connecting and collaborating with others, on your own terms, in your own context, developing your own plan of action, doing your own thing in sync, in community, with others. It does require knowing yourself first: Knowing your personal Gift, Passion, and Purpose.

To discover the partners you seek, it probably won't suffice to rely solely on Web sites, databases, or other online technologies. You need to draw on a broader pool of talent and passion, including those who don't use these technologies.

Likewise, you're unlikely to find the right partners through business incubators or other venture-partner agencies. As James Surowiecki has explained,[5] the agent gets rewarded for making connections, and for that reason she or he will always be tempted to exaggerate the potential of every relationship.

A more effective, low-tech, peer-to-peer approach might be:

Articulate Unmet Needs (That You Care About): Don't begin with a proposal or manifesto of what you think is the answer. Instead, table a problem, approach it with an open mind and as much data as possible, and engage others to help solve it. Probe the need, substantiate it with evidence, and discuss it extensively. Students of complex systems know that an understanding of the problem co-evolves with the emergence of possible solutions, so what is important is to *articulate the problem or need,* *and not rush to solutions.* The process of finding and articulating unmet needs is further explained in Chapter 3.

Find Others Who Share Your Sense of Purpose: Your Purpose is what you were always meant to do, why you're here. It's personal, and the articulation and discussion of needs connected to that Purpose will draw in people who share it. This is not a persuasive process—you're appealing to the latent interest that people already have in the subject. Those who respond will bring additional knowledge to improve the understanding of the need. Consider crafting an invitation[6] to an event focused on discussing solutions to this need that draws in even more people.

Identify Prospective Partners: Some of those you draw in to discuss these unmet needs will be prospective Partners, people who share your Purpose and have Gifts and Passions complementary to your own. In the process of brainstorming approaches to the needs, you'll have a basis to assess how you might work with these people in a Natural Enterprise. And in the process, you'll learn more about the needs and problems you're grappling with and evolve better potential solutions.

Another approach is to set aside your Gift and Passion and Purpose for a while and start with the people you think you'd love to work with.

Starting with who you think you'd like to work with

Knowing where your Gift and Passion intersect is helpful in providing focus to your search for natural work—it helps you to set aside self-indulgences (things you love but are not acknowledged as very good at by others) and unfulfilling options (things you're acknowledged as very good at, but don't really have any passion for).

Finding the sweet spot, however, requires us to get away from our comfort zones, our regular routines, what we know, and explore some areas that appeal to us but that are uncharted territory. Volunteering is one way to do that. Travel is another.

But instead of starting with what you think you might want to do, what about starting with *who you'd like to do it with*? My top advice to aspiring entrepreneurs is not to try to start a business yourself. The biggest problem with navel-gazing around Gift, Passion, and Purpose is that it may get you thinking about working alone, doing it all yourself. Maybe the perfect work for you is working as a partner *in an enterprise that does things that are wildly beyond your personal competencies and even knowledge*, but that draws on your Gifts and Passions in ways that are essential to the Enterprise.

So suppose you start by answering the question: *Of all the people I know and think I would like to know, who would I most like to work with?* Then maybe you need to think about some possibilities of work that you might want to do with them. Or maybe not—maybe the next step is just to call them up and say:

> Start by answering the question: *Of all the people I know and think I would like to know, who would I most like to work with?*

> "I've decided I would like to work with you. I think together we would be a force to be reckoned with. We have some complementary strengths and interests, and I think the chemistry between us would be good. I have no idea what we would do, but my instincts tell me whatever it was, it would be successful, and a lot of fun. What do you think of the idea of getting together and talking it over?"

Scary thought, perhaps. Imagine writing or phoning people you don't know but have always admired! This is a bit like screwing up the courage to ask someone you have had a secret crush on for a date. What if the people you'd like to work with are already working for someone else, seemingly happy or at least committed to their current jobs? What if you don't even *know* who you might like to make a living with—where and how do you start to look?

Think of it like looking for any other kind of partner—a potential spouse or date. Yes, we all know "the best ones are already taken," but that doesn't mean they aren't looking for something better, something that fills that empty place inside. I think you'd be surprised how many people working hard at respectable jobs would be flattered, and perhaps very interested, in exploring opportunities that could let them find the work at the intersections of their Passions, Gifts, and Purposes.

> You'd be surprised how many people working hard at respectable jobs would be flattered and interested in opportunities that could let them find the work at the intersections of their Passions, Gifts, and Purposes.

And as long as you're just sitting there, what harm would it do to ask? The worst that could happen is they'll say "no."

And if they say "yes," then what?

Then you change the task from finding how your (singular) Passions and Gifts can find their Purpose, to finding how your (plural) Passions and collective Gifts can find their Purpose, together.

Again, it's an iterative process that can start with Gifts, Passions, or identified needs. Let's suppose you have identified a group of twenty to thirty people you want to start a Natural Enterprise with.

You could start with a Gift Inventory—group members identify their Gifts, what they're uniquely good at, and how they know (e.g., recognition and appreciation by someone else). If others who know that person can chime in, that's helpful, too. Preparing the collective Gift Inventory could be quite eye-opening: Some people might discover their Gifts for the first time, or even discover that what they thought were their Gift actually weren't.

I think it makes sense if you start with the Gift Inventory to then look at what's needed (collective Purpose). This would require both group brainstorming and lots of research by everyone in the group. Most of all, it involves candor about the things each of you really cares about.

The research into needs must be *primary*—face-to-face conversations with potential customers to gather as much information as possible about possible needs, not online research. If the need is obvious out there in cyberspace, chances are someone's already filling it. Primary research gives you information that's yours alone.

Once you've identified a bunch of possible needs that would appear to fit with the group's collective Gifts, the next step would be to reconvene the group to discuss them. This is entrepreneurship 101: Articulating the market need(s) as precisely as possible, and crafting (this is art, not science) offerings that appear to meet all the specifications of these needs. Then you need to do two things simultaneously: self-identify the people in the group who have the Gifts needed to provide those offerings, and ensure that those people would be Passionate about their roles—that it's something that they would love to do.

This is tricky, and there are several land mines to watch out for. You may find that there's too much overlap in the group's Gifts, and there is not room for everyone in the group in an enterprise providing this offering. There may be more than one offering identified in the session, which may solve this problem, but the last thing you need in a new enterprise is too much of a particular talent—the result will likely be infighting, turf wars, and disengagement.

You may find that there are gaps that no one in the group has a Gift for, in which case you'll need to find others to join the group— others you want to make a living with. A mistake traditional enterprises often make is recruiting outsiders strictly for their talent, even though they may be obnoxious, have poor chemistry with the rest of the group, and have no particular Passion for what the business is doing. They're like the free-agent superstars in professional sports— their teams are often not as successful as teams with less talent but more cohesion and mutual love.

You may find that you have the collective Gifts and a dynamite offering, but that some people in the group just don't have the Passion to make a living around that offering. An entire enterprise doing work they don't have Passion for, brilliantly, will be a workplace of resentment and restlessness—and what a tragedy to have people who love each other working together doing stuff they hate! You cannot compromise on your or your partners' Passions. Go back to your research and find a need your group really cares about, with work they can really enjoy, not just do well.

Another approach: Starting with your Passions

So that's how this process might work starting with collective Gifts. Could the iteration start with collective Passions, or needs, instead?

A lot of entrepreneurial businesses do start with collective Passions. I've seen a lot of them fail because the team lacks the requisite Gifts, or because their Gifts overlap too much or have a lot of competency gaps that end up being filled by disinterested mercenaries. Or because their Passion gets in the way of realizing that there is no acknowledged, practical market need for their offering, or because their offering is not affordable. Solutions in search of a problem. As important as Passion is, I don't think it's the best place to start this process, at least not when you're doing it at a collective level.

Getting the people you want to make a living with to focus *collectively* on identifying an unmet need, though, is a viable alternative to starting with collective Gifts. Again, thorough, disciplined primary research is needed to identify a set of unmet needs. Something you *think* is needed is not enough to start with. You need to learn why something you think is needed is not already being provided by someone else—the market is not perfect, but it tends to fill big obvious gaps quickly and effectively. Once you know why the need isn't being filled, you need to be brutally honest about whether and how you can circumvent the obstacle that is preventing others from filling it. The most likely answer is that the niche is currently too small to be commercial.

This is the entré of most successful new enterprises—what Christensen calls disruptive innovations (more on this in Chapter 4): Starting small and getting really good really fast so that the niche you're filling gets much broader and catches the incumbent businesses napping.

If I were coordinating a group trying to establish a Natural Enterprise together, I'd start with either (a) a general type of problem or (b) a target customer segment. Then I'd teach the group how to do good research, and a bit about disruptive innovation, and have them both individually (one-on-one primary research) and collectively (brainstorming) produce a whole set of unmet needs around that particular problem or customer segment.

For example, if the problem was "the End of Oil," the objective might be to find a whole set of possible renewable energy offerings. Or, if the target underserved customer segment was "local communities," the objective might be to find a whole set of possible offerings that are focused on the needs of local communities (like creating local organic food networks, or creating markets for local artists, craftspeople, and/or tradespeople).

These would need to be problems or underserved customer segments that you believe the group has some collective Passion about, so in a way you *are* starting with Passion—but not with what the people in your group love doing, rather who they would love to do it *for* (i.e., what customer group) or *why* they would love doing it (i.e., what problem that they care about would it solve).

This does not guarantee the group will end up passionate about the resultant offering. For example, I'd love to be involved in a renewable energy business or a local organic food network, but not as its accountant, even though that's where my Gift in that enterprise may lie. *Passion for the purpose is not the same as Passion for the role.*

So now suppose you've compiled a set of well-researched, unmet needs. When the group reconvenes, the group members can then address how to address those needs by considering each person's Gifts and Passions simultaneously. In other words, after you start by defining the group's Purpose (i.e., what unmet needs it will fill), then you have each person declare how his or her Gifts could contribute to that enterprise, in a way that he or she would be Passionate about doing so.

For example, I may be able to contribute to a renewable energy business in many ways (finding financing for it, teaching other members about the science and markets for renewable energy, etc.) but the way in which I could contribute that I'd be most Passionate about is creatively identifying and exploring all the options that are available, and how they vary by community, and putting together a set of "templates" that could be customized to the needs and available sources of renewable energy in each community so that the business would offer different but appropriate services to each community in which it operated.

That role taps into both my imaginative Gifts and my Passion for discovery.

Like the first approach, this approach to finding the sweet spot is tricky and full of land mines. Some people may reluctantly admit that they just have no Gift or Passion for the new enterprise that the group collectively creates, and have to opt out. There may again be overlaps or gaps in the Gifts. And although some people may be passionate about the Purpose of the enterprise, they may reluctantly conclude that they don't have Passion for the only role that is appropriate for them to play in it.

This is the epitome of complexity, which is why it is so important for the people involved in the process to love each other and to really want to work together. Participants probably will learn as much about themselves and others in the group as they will about business, needs, and markets. This is not an exercise for wallflowers!

In summary, I think there are two optimal routes for a whole group of people who want to make a living together to iteratively find the sweet spot where their collective Gifts and Passions and unmet needs intersect:

- Start with an Inventory of collective Gifts of a group of people who'd love to work together, then research unmet needs that draw on those Gifts, and then assess each person's Passion for applying those Gifts to those needs.
- Or, start with a Purpose the group is passionate about (solving a particular problem or helping a particular underserved customer segment), then research unmet needs that are related to that problem or shared by that underserved segment, and then assess each person's Gift and Passion for addressing those unmet needs.

If this were easy, we would all be doing it intuitively. Its complexity is the reason most of us are unhappy, incompetent, or unsuccessful at what we're doing, and working with people we are indifferent to, or worse. When we wait for others to take the initiative, to "offer us" a job, we either wait forever, or settle for much less than we had hoped for.

So identify the people you think you'd love to make a living with, call them up, and invite them to explore possibilities. What have you got to lose?

As I stated at the start of this chapter, finding the right partners is challenging, and there are no simple methods or silver-bullet approaches.

The Web site that accompanies this book, Finding Natural Partners http://NaturalEnterprise.org/partners/, continues this chapter's conversation. It lets you share your Gifts, Passions, and Purpose with others, and discover how others have found the people they were meant to make a living with, and how they found them, and what mistakes people have made in this quest that we can all learn from. I hope to see it evolve, with readers' and entrepreneurs' help, into a service that will make this important challenge a little easier. Like a dating service, but with a modestly different purpose, and without the cheesy videos.

These first two chapters have explained the hardest part of Natural Entrepreneurship—discovering what you were meant to make a living doing, and who you were meant to do it with.

The next two chapters explain what you and your partners must do next: Research the unmet needs that you can uniquely fill and craft the solutions that fill those needs. I'll explain how the best researchers and the best innovators differentiate themselves from the rest of the pack, and why these two processes can be done much more powerfully and effectively by Natural Enterprises than by traditional corporations.

So now, sit down with your newly found natural partners and learn these two essential entrepreneurial skills together.

CHAPTER 2 CASE STUDY
A shared Purpose of service: "To be of use"

Briarpatch

Briarpatch Cooperative Market was a Natural Enterprise started by serial entrepreneur Dave Smith. Its success is documented in Dave's book *To Be of Use*[7], and mentioned in his Foreword to this book.

"In the midst of our everyday work," he writes, "we may give pause and wonder why so much of it is love-*less,* meaning-*less.*" Briarpatch was an exception to this. It was started by a group of people who knew and trusted each other, and who shared a passion for good, wholesome food at a reasonable cost, and for doing meaningful work with people they loved.

The cooperative ran on fully egalitarian principles of working together that were "open, inclusive, cooperative, service-oriented, hardworking, supportive, effective, meaningful, and fun to be in. And no one woke up the next morning dreading the work day."

One of the operating principles that they embraced was the notion of stewardship outlined in Peter Block's book *Stewardship* [8], where it is defined as "the willingness to be accountable for the well-being of the larger organization by operating in service, rather than in control, of those around us."

Eventually the members of Briarpatch caught the Silicon Valley wave and the co-op disbanded, gracefully, paying off its few debts when it closed. But the lessons and experiences of Briarpatch have guided and influenced Dave and his partners in his many entrepreneurial ventures since.

Dave discovered, through his work with Briarpatch and subsequent Natural Enterprises, that much of industrial agriculture is based on dangerous myths, and set out to smash those myths and create a model that was more honest, responsible, and sustainable.

As a result, Dave was asked to serve as a director of Diamond Organics, a company that employed organic financing. The company, which now sells more than $3 million worth of organic foods each year, raised $1 million in capital entirely from 150 customers. These customers are patient and committed to the company and its principles, not obsessed with Return on Investment. Now that the company is doing so well, some of this money has been advanced organically to other small companies "doing good for the world."

. . . .

CHAPTER 2 CASE STUDY
A shared Purpose of ecological responsibility

Mountain Equipment Co-op

"As a co-operative, MEC exists to serve the needs of our members. Our products are built with purpose, people, and the planet in mind. . . . Count on us to act with integrity. We're driven by passion, not profit. We continue to look for ways to protect our wild spaces and reduce the ecological footprint of our business."

So begins the Web site of Canada's Mountain Equipment Co-op, a company whose every decision is dictated by Natural Enterprise principles. Some examples include:

- Every product is built to last. Durability, not fashion, is the landmark of the company's products.
- Their goal is to make affordable, quality products for the outdoors, and that their gear be made in a way that respects the people who manufacture it. Through its Ethical Sourcing Program, MEC works toward creating safer working conditions, legal working hours, and reasonable pay for work done.
- MEC chooses lower impact materials and production techniques to reduce its ecological footprint on the planet. Materials include recycled polyester and organic cotton. They recycle all

their garments themselves, and use no harmful PVCs in any of their materials.

- Their community-involvement program is a comprehensive grant and partnership program that supports Canadian wilderness conservation and recreational access initiatives.
- Their award-winning "Green Building" program reduces energy consumption by 50 percent over conventional retail and manufacturing space, and savings are invested in global warming awareness and mitigation programs.
- New products are innovated in collaboration with customers and employees who field-test experimental new designs and continuously improve them until they're ready for market.
- New product design must conform to the members' six operating principles: accountability, quality, inspiration, appropriate use of resources and technology, simplicity, and responsibility to members, society, and the environment.
- The company is involved in dozens of community-improvement partnerships. One of these is Leave No Trace, an ethical program for outdoor recreation that MEC's employees master and teach in the community.
- One percent of all sales are donated to environmental causes.

PART TWO

CREATING NATURAL WORK

FINDING UNMET NEEDS TO FILL
conducting extraordinary research

Research is to see what everybody else has seen, and to think what nobody else has thought

—Nobel scientist Albert Szent-Gyorgyi

There is nothing like looking, if you want to find something. You certainly usually find something, if you look, but it is not always quite the something you were after.

—J. R. R. Tolkien

Part One of this book described a process for discovering what you were meant to do and finding the right partners to do it with. This second part describes a process for deciding what your Natural Enterprise is going to be about—what it will do and how it will do it.

As I have mentioned before, the entire process of finding natural work is an iterative one—once you've homed in on what your enterprise will be about, you may find it changes your perspective on what you were meant to do, or who you should ideally do it with. What's important is to cover all six steps in the process—there is no one right order in which to do them.

This chapter will help you decide what your Natural Enterprise will do—initially, and continuously as it evolves. We'll revisit Morgana, Janis, and Jean-Paul's Really Simple Technologies enterprise to explore how they might do their research and what unmet needs it might bring to the surface.

This process starts with understanding what's needed and how those needs fit with your enterprise's collective Purpose.

Find a need and fill it.

Most traditional businesses have large research and development (R&D) departments, as well as marketing and promotion departments created to convince customers to buy the products they invent. In these companies, R&D would more properly be called "new product development"—the company decides on a product that is within its competencies to make, and makes it. It's assumed that if the decision-makers in the company like the idea, then so will customers.

I've seen first-time entrepreneurs approach their businesses the same way. They have some idea for a product or service that *they* would love to buy, and assume that everyone else would want it too. They invest huge efforts and expense in developing the product or service and bringing it to market, and then are devastated to find that there is no market for it.

> **Most successful entrepreneurs start with potential customers, explore with them what *they* need, discover why that need is not already being met in the market, and *then* develop their product or service.**

The most successful entrepreneurs I know approach product development in a more natural way: They start with potential customers, explore with them what *they* need, discover why that need is not already being met in the market, and *then* develop their product or service.

Many of the most entrepreneurial organizations in the world have adopted this approach, and continue to use it, investing more, and earlier, in customer and market research, and less in marketing and the R&D "laboratory."

MIT's entrepreneurial guru Michael Dertouzos writes:

> Perhaps the most important ingredient of successful innovation is the creative technological idea that serves a pressing human need. This kind of creativity, in turn, requires a schizophrenic combination of rationality and insanity that's outside our ordinary experience. Imagine that all current

inventions in the world and all their possible logical extensions and uses are inside a huge balloon. People are pretty good at extending these ideas further, using logic and common sense. But their results, being logical extensions of what's already there, stay within the balloon. To escape these old ideas and come up with something that is radically new, the balloon must be punctured with something that defies reason ... striving to zero in on the key ingredient—a creative idea that serves a pressing human need.[1]

What does this mean?

You know you're using a natural approach to business research and development if:

1. The offerings of the enterprise fill unmet business, social, or consumer needs.
2. The enterprise understood why those needs weren't already being met and overcame those obstacles.
3. The enterprise has the competencies and resources to effectively create and deliver offerings that fill those needs.

This may sound like a simple recipe, but it's actually quite difficult to achieve. The market for products and services, although far from perfect, is reasonably efficient at identifying and satisfying needs. If you find an unmet need, there is almost surely a reason why that need isn't being met by some other enterprise.

You need to find out what that reason is, and overcome it—if it *can* be overcome. (You may conclude there's no economically feasible way to overcome it, in which case you'll have to look for some other unmet need to fill.)

And then you and your partners need to ensure you have the collective Gifts and capacities required to design, produce, market, and distribute the product or service that meets that need and the resources (physical, financial, and intellectual) needed to do so effectively. Easier said than done.

What's more, people often don't *know* what they need. An iterative, exploratory approach to observing and interviewing potential customers must be used to unearth unmet and *unrealized* needs. Deep, continuous relationships with these customers are needed to sustain the realization of additional unmet needs as the enterprise evolves to fill them. These relationships are sometimes so intimate that the customers essentially codevelop new products and services with the enterprise.

> **The key is *research*, the difficult, time-consuming (but usually inexpensive) process of discovering the who, what, when, where, why, and how of unmet needs.**

The key to doing this is *research*, the difficult, time-consuming (but usually inexpensive) process of discovering the who, what, when, where, why, and how of unmet needs.

In this chapter, we're going to look at a research process that naturally allows you do this.

The research process

This research process has eight steps. The first six steps enable you to find unmet needs, while the last two enable you to "qualify" whether these needs are ones your Natural Enterprise can and should fill.

Step 1: Identify your customers

The first step in identifying unmet needs is answering the question: *Whose needs?*

The answer to this question should not be hard to find if you start with the collective, shared Purpose that you and your Natural Enterprise partners have discovered.

The shared purpose that the partners of Really Simple Technologies, our case study from the last chapter, agreed upon was:

Invent, develop, and deploy simple, inexpensive technologies that will reduce greenhouse gases, reduce oil dependency, and enable nations to become more self-sufficient.

RST's partners, Janis, Morgana, and Jean-Paul, in commencing their search for unmet needs they can fill, need to research and talk through who would buy these technologies. They might decide that governments, large emitters of greenhouse gases, public foundations, alternative energy entrepreneurs, and end consumers in rich and poor

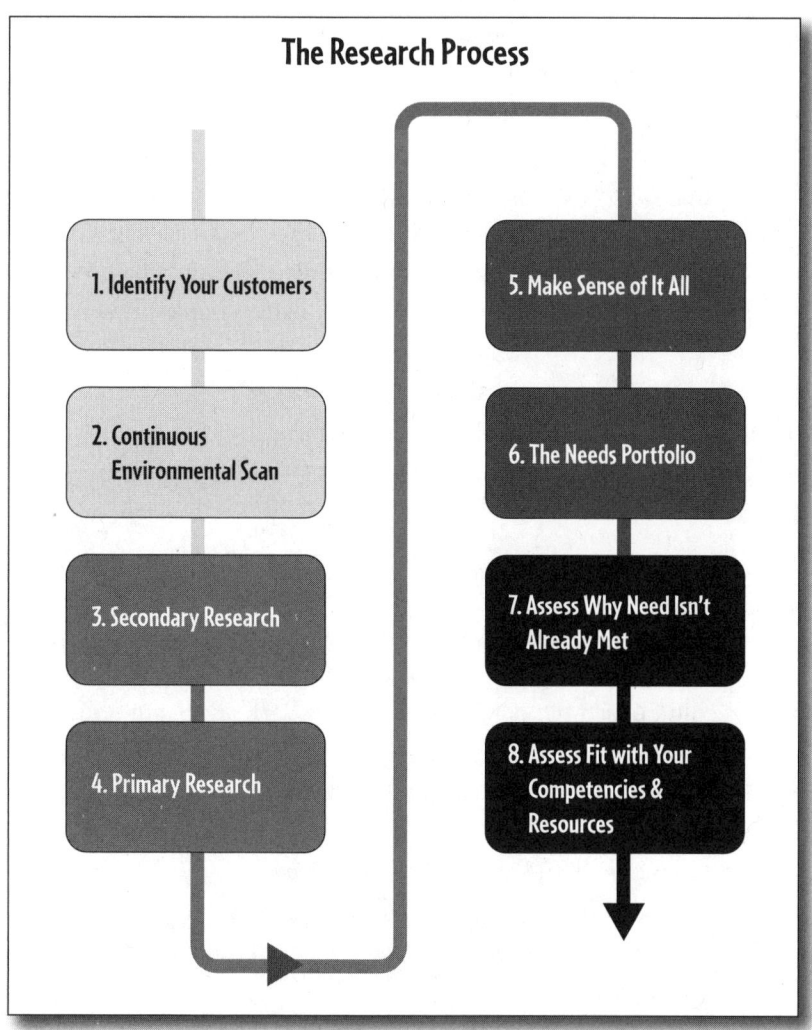

The Research Process

1. Identify Your Customers

2. Continuous Environmental Scan

3. Secondary Research

4. Primary Research

5. Make Sense of It All

6. The Needs Portfolio

7. Assess Why Need Isn't Already Met

8. Assess Fit with Your Competencies & Resources

countries might *all* be customers for *some* of their products. As they begin to develop specific products, this assessment might evolve, but it's important from the outset to decide who your customers are.

In business circles, this is often called "segmentation" of your customers—breaking them into groups that share certain needs, what they have in common (affinities), and buying behaviors. In the natural process of codeveloping your products with your customers, you will select a small group of customers who will represent each of the segments of your identified customer market. This small group of "surrogate" customers is called *the pathfinders.* In your primary research (step 4 of the research process) these pathfinder customers are going to be your principal source of intelligence on the unmet needs you are trying to fill. You will be spending a lot of time with these pathfinders. They will show you the path to meet their unmet needs, and will be your allies as you create your Natural Enterprise.

Don't expect to get the segments perfect right away. As you explore your pathfinders' needs, affinities, and buying behaviors, you probably will change the makeup of your pathfinder group.

Step 2: Continuous environmental scan

The next step in the research process is setting up a continuous environmental scan. This involves continuous monitoring for news and information about:

- the economy
- the political and regulatory situation
- new technologies, inventions, and innovations
- cultural, artistic, demographic, attitudinal, and labor shifts and trends
- scientific (including nature) discoveries
- social and environmental attitudes and developments
- commodities and materials developments
- the competitive landscape, including new suppliers, customers, competitors, materials, substitute products, and marketing and pricing trends

The scanning process includes capturing, filtering, analyzing, and disseminating information. Many organizations now use a combination of RSS feeds[2] and other subscriptions, along with keyword alerts and other alerting services, to aggregate the information they need.

This scan produces essential raw material for your secondary and primary research, and the sense-making process that follows (steps 3–5 below).

Here's a methodology for continuous environmental scanning one of my clients uses that seems to work well:

Know how you learn: Understand your "information behavior." Some people like information "pushed" to them through e-mails. Others like to go out and "pull" this information from an RSS aggregator page when they're ready for it. Design your continuous environmental scan for your and your partners' preference. Be prepared to offer the results in both push and pull "flavors."

Determine your information universe: Spend some time (and brainstorm with others) to identify the universe of different sources you want your scan "radar" to capture. Note that Google News doesn't capture all news sources, and most other news aggregators capture only a very few select media sources. Make a complete list of all the news sources that are of interest to you—the raw newswires, local, national, and international newspapers and media Web sites, magazines and trade periodicals, newsletters, analyst reports, technology analysts, scientific and technology news, blogs, demographic research studies, and economic news sources. Some useful sources may not be available online, and others are available only for a fee. If you're doing this for business, don't forget to scan industries that could be developing new processes, technologies, and innovations that could affect your industry. Don't forget to track new books on your favorite subjects, as well as multimedia sources such as radio programs, TV documentaries, training materials, and so on.

Discover infomediaries: Consider how you can tap into others who already are aggregating some of the content you care about. Trade and industry associations often summarize relevant news on their Web sites and newsletters. There are many specialized bloggers: Just Google the topic or industry you're interested in and the word "blog" and you'll be amazed at what you'll find. Check out online bookmarking tools such as del.icio.us that tag news by subject—it's like accessing thousands of specialized librarians free of charge. There are some excellent cross-disciplinary e-newsletters out there as well. Some of these "infomediaries" include summaries, free of charge, of articles from other sources that they've paid for. Most of them offer RSS feeds.

Tap into your partners and their networks: Survey what your Natural Enterprise partners, and the people in their networks, have on their hard drives and subscription lists, and devise ways to have these feed into your environmental scan.

Filter and channel this content: Now that you have the content for the top of the funnel, the next step is to filter it. How you do that will depend on the format it is in and the tools at your disposal. Learn to write terse, one-sentence abstracts of articles, one-paragraph summaries of books, and put them at the front, to save rereading to remember what it was about. Learn to write short two- or three-page summaries of books for those who should, but won't, read the whole thing. Once you've organized it by subject and filtered and abstracted the content, split it into "channels" by topic and subtopic and use RSS to allow your partners and others to "subscribe" to the channels that most interest them. You'll probably find one or two of your Natural Enterprise partners will have more energy and affinity for this sorting, summarizing, organizing, and channeling work—let them do it.

Even if you have identified and qualified some blockbuster unmet needs to start your Natural Enterprise, a continuous environmental scan can help bring to the surface new needs that will sustain the enterprise over the longer term.

Step 3: Secondary research

There are two kinds of research: *Secondary* research entails reading and browsing online to gather information that has already been published about the market, and need, and the possible solutions to it. *Primary* research entails talking to people directly to answer these questions, gathering unpublished information and intelligence.

How do you go about doing this? To some extent it will depend, of course, on what your enterprise is all about. You're going to have to be creative, patient, and methodical in solving the all-important problem of identifying what the market needs and understanding why these needs are not already being satisfied by existing products and services. That means you're going to have to take the time to learn a lot about the marketplace and about customers.

Here are four categories of ideas and areas to explore to get you thinking about possible unmet needs for secondary research:

Changes and Trends
What's changing?: Look at changes and trends in the marketplace from consumer attitudes to buying behaviors: What's hot, and what new needs will the demand for suddenly hot products and services spawn? How is the market responding to changing consumption patterns?

What's being transformed?: What's happening to transform certain industries or economic sectors, such as education, public health, and even defense, and how might those transformational ideas, products, processes, technologies, and models be applied in other industries and economic sectors?

What's time has come?: What great ideas failed, and why? Maybe they were ahead of their time, and their time is now.

Problems That Need Solving
What's wrong?: What are people complaining about? Every complaint reflects an unmet need.

What's keeping business leaders awake?: What problems are businesses facing? What could you offer that would let them sleep better?

What's being neglected?: What small "niches of need" exist in consumer markets that big, unspecialized businesses can't be bothered to satisfy?

What's not working?: Look around you at the problems you and your peers struggle with every day. For example, I keep hearing that the number-one cause of laptop failures is the power cord and the power supply, and in particular the connection between the two. This is a high stress point, with cords constantly being pulled, bent and folded, and that flimsy connection takes the brunt of this stress. It's a terrible design, and a crucial unmet need that Apple recognized; they now provide magnetic connectors on their laptops (reducing stress and wear, and preventing potential damage to the machine when people trip over the cord). Why haven't other suppliers come up with a similar solution?

Things That Are Missing

What's lacking?: What do people think there's never enough of? Sustained shortages represent business opportunities.

Where are the gaps?: What are the gaps in products and services? In *The Support Economy*,[3] Shoshana Zuboff describes the next economy as one where the customer's needs are met "end-to-end." People don't have time or patience to fill in the product and service gaps, like when the great product breaks down and there's no backup, or when the daycare service closes two hours before they get home from work. A gap implies an unmet need.

What could be added?: Is there a new service that you could "wrap around" an existing product or service to make it more valuable? (Offering haircuts and rinses in people's homes and offices, or dinner on the commuter train, for example.)

Untapped Opportunities

What's unexpected but possible?: In *Innovation and Entrepreneurship*,[4] the late Peter Drucker identified seven areas of innovation opportunity resulting from discontinuities, all of which can be used to unearth unmet needs:

1. *Unexpected occurrences* (If there's a dramatic change in government, what new market opportunities will that present?)

2. *Perception/reality incongruities* (When greenhouse gases bring about massive climate and environmental change in our lifetimes, how will customer needs change?)

3. *Process weaknesses or needs* (Some believe advertising has no future: if they're right, what will business need in order to get information to customers in other ways?)

4. *Industry and market changes* (What will $160/barrel oil mean to us all?)

5. *Demographic changes* (What will the huge number of people retiring in the next ten to twenty years do with their time?)

6. *Buyers' attitude and priority changes* (Consumers see file-sharing as a work-around for CD price-gouging, and TiVo as the solution to lousy program offerings and excess commercials—what does that mean for these industries?)

7. *New scientific and business knowledge* (How will RFID devices change the way we live, shop, and work, and protect or interfere with our privacy?)

What's essential to human happiness?: Look at basic, overarching human needs: Health, safety, education, time, decent quality of life, meaning, recreation. How are our experiences of these things currently unsatisfactory, and how might they be improved?

What's needed somewhere else?: Is there a market somewhere in the world for something we take for granted but they don't have at all? And vice versa, do people in some other countries take for granted things that we have never considered selling here? In Europe, for example, some movie theaters offer excellent cuisine and fine wine—would that work in North America?

If you think about the great inventions of all time, most of them were devised to address a deep-seated human need. Controlled fire, the arrowhead, agriculture, animal domestication, paper, political, educational and economic systems, money, artificial light, electricity, the engine, and language all evolved remarkably quickly to meet emerging, urgent needs.

Our modern age once again presents a host of new, deep human needs: The need for ways to cope with epidemic disease, crime and pollution, global warming, and other problems caused by ever increasing human numbers living ever more extravagantly in ever closer proximity. The need for ways to power all our equipment and heat our homes when we run out of cheap hydrocarbons and dam-able rivers. The need for ways to combat poverty, corruption, and the hugely inequitable distribution of wealth and power.

All these needs cry out for imaginative, innovative, practical, affordable solutions. Some of them are likely to be "on Purpose" for your Natural Enterprise—consistent with what you and your partners feel you were meant to make a living at, together.

The paradox of research and invention is that needs are sometimes not recognized until a solution to them has been developed. This is especially true of new technologies that have provided people with the ability to do things (such as listen to music, watch videos, or converse) anywhere, any time, that previously had to be done at a particular time and place. Now we feel we need this ability, but until the capacity to provide it was

> The paradox of research and invention is that needs are sometimes not recognized until a solution to them has been developed.

invented, we didn't. It takes great imagination and a deep understanding of potential customers to develop solutions as needs for them are co-evolving and emerging in the complex social and economic fabric of everyday life.

Many of the problems and needs that have prevailed throughout our civilization are clustered in four areas: health, education, personal communication, and recreation.

All four of these areas are deeply personal, rooted in needs at the base of the Maslow[5] human-needs hierarchy. Look at the issues that elections are fought and won on, and these are usually at the top.

Look at what most government and personal money is spent on and you'll find these four areas rank high in every budget.

Many of the problems in these areas are intractable—they are complex and have eluded attempts to solve them using any institutional or standardized approach. Trillions have been spent on them and still the needs remain.

These four areas are rich mines to explore in your search for unmet needs.

The resource guide at the end of this book provides links to some articles I have written that will help unearth and reveal additional unmet needs that may be "on Purpose" for your Natural Enterprise, by doing secondary research on:

- Intractable problems that no one has found satisfactory answers for,
- Needs right in your local community,
- New needs that have emerged in the twenty-first century,
- Needs that come to light by learning to "pay constant attention."

This secondary research is something you should do as much as possible with your Natural Enterprise partners. It is the conversation and interchange of ideas that comes from doing this research that allows a collective understanding of possible unmet needs you can meet to emerge from the huge amount of information you must wade through in your secondary research.

Step 4: Primary research

Some people call this approach "shoe-leather" research because, unlike secondary research, primary research needs to be done face-to-face, and you need to get away from your computer and library and listen to pathfinders, other customers, business allies, and others, and wear out some shoe leather to do it.

Primary research involves a variety of techniques: interviews, surveys (with open-ended questions), observation, studying the need personally, seeing what others are doing or have tried to do to meet the need, and just engaging in conversations, listening, and paying attention. Ideally, this should always be done face-to-face, with the telephone used only to obtain appointments, at least unless and until you know the interviewee well.

You may be surprised to discover how generous people are with their time and attention when you do this. People love to offer their opinions when they think the person asking for it really cares about their answers. If you're genuine and enthusiastic, you can gather extremely valuable and reliable information this way, *information you cannot get any other way, and that no one else will have.*

All it takes is time, patience, skill at asking the right questions and paying attention to the answers, and wearing out a lot of shoe leather. There is no shortcut for this. Secondary, online research is never enough.

Along the way, you'll also learn a lot about the research process, and you'll get better and faster at it the more you persevere. I know researchers who have become the de facto subject-matter experts on a lot of subjects in their industries, far more informed, and better able to substantiate their opinions, than the gurus who have worked in the industry all their lives. Good primary researchers have the benefit of current information gleaned directly from the horses' mouths, a lot of them—the Wisdom of Crowds.

This research can dramatically reduce the amount of time, effort, and money you need to spend promoting and marketing your product or service. (You've already met a lot of your first customers, and if you fill their unmet needs, they will spread the word to others—and take some pride in having played a part in your success.) It can even reduce the amount of money you need to raise to launch the enterprise.

But most importantly, you should follow this process, grueling as it may be, because it works. If you doubt me, talk to any successful entrepreneur about the value of doing this, and you'll be convinced.

Recently, I've seen several presentations that use a four-approach model to understanding prospective customers and their needs.

It seems to work because, depending on their *worldview*, sensitivities, drivers, and biases, different people are engaged, informed, and persuaded by different things: Some respond better to negatives (threats, risks) and others to positives (benefits, opportunities).

And depending on their *context* for understanding the problem or issue, different people have different levels of knowledge and awareness about it: By taking different approaches to understanding human problems and needs, we appeal to different understandings and contexts, at least one of which should work for each person you interview. So when you're interviewing your pathfinders, and deciding what to ask to unearth their unmet needs, consider probing using each of these four approaches.

The four approaches are:

Anxieties: What is causing stress to your interviewee? People who respond to this approach are those who focus on the urgent before the important. If an issue is keeping them awake at night, they will have a propensity to listen and respond positively to ideas and proposals that might address it. Asking people what they're most worried about is one way to identify unmet needs.

Incapabilities: What can your interviewee not currently do that they want to be able to do? People who respond to this approach are those who focus on vulnerabilities rather than abilities. If an issue makes them feel that they are at risk if they do not resolve it, they will have a propensity to listen and respond positively to ideas and proposals that address it, even if the benefits are otherwise small. So asking people what they wish they could do, or do better, is another way to identify unmet needs.

Emotional needs: What does your interviewee ache for, long for? People who are very emotional or needy will respond to ideas and proposals that address emotional wants and needs that they already have identified and perhaps articulated, which to their knowledge cannot be met by any obvious solution. You engage such people by understanding the emotions that drive them and recognizing and anticipating what they need and want, without them having to tell you.

Benefits: What are the specific, measurable benefits to your interviewee of ideas that you have been thinking about? Some people are impressed more by opportunity than risk, and will respond to ideas and proposals that stress benefits that they can personally relate to in the context of doing their jobs, tasks, or hobbies. Some people are excellent "sounding boards" for ideas when their benefits are presented, and from the benefits they respond to, the needs that underlie them can be deduced.

As you can imagine, the process of finding unmet needs is an iterative one. You cannot just go up to people and ask them what they need and expect a coherent, meaningful, or insightful answer.

In the process of talking to people (primary research), you quickly will discover an important truth: *People don't know what they need.* That is why "marketing surveys" are so ineffective at identifying needs. It requires *conversation* to ascertain what people need. It's a back-and-forth between ideas, possibilities, approaches (the first steps toward solutions to needs), and articulation of those needs themselves.

This chapter and the one that follows (on imagining possibilities and the innovation process) are closely linked because the process of identifying unmet needs is a *complex* process: *the understanding of the problem or need co-evolves with the emergence of possible solutions.*

As you articulate a possible idea, answer, or approach, the people you speak with will gain a deeper understanding of what they really need. And as they articulate their need more coherently, additional ideas, answers, and approaches will come to mind, will emerge from the conversation.

There is a definite skill to such conversations, but it is one that

> As you articulate a possible idea, answer, or approach, the people you speak with will gain a deeper understanding of what they really need. As they articulate their need more coherently, additional ideas, answers, and approaches will emerge from the conversation.

we almost all have inherently—the human species is by nature a problem-solving species. And this is how we solve problems—by allowing our understanding of the problem and our appreciation of possible solutions to co-evolve and to co-emerge.

There are four special techniques for doing primary research that, in my experience, are particularly effective: Cultural Anthropology, Thinking the Customer Ahead Sessions, Wisdom of Crowds Survey, and Open Space Events.

Step 4a: Customer Anthropology

Customer Anthropology is observing customers (and potential customers) at work as a means of discovering unmet needs that your enterprise can fill. You won't read much about it on the Web because it's still competitive-advantage stuff: What I know about the science of it I cannot disclose under a confidentiality agreement, and most of the companies doing it (Steelcase, Intel, Volkswagen, Microsoft) aren't talking about it much.

Although I can't talk about the science, I can talk about the art, and anyone who's a decent observer with a critical mind can quickly devise their own methodology for doing it from that.

If you're a birdwatcher—one who's really into animal behavior and not just ticking another species off on your list—you're halfway there. Customer Anthropology is a lot like birdwatching in that you want to try to make yourself invisible to those you're watching—you want to see what they would do if you weren't there, not witness their performance for you.

That means that you need to get permission to observe your customers and put them at ease. From experience I can tell you that getting permission is easier than it sounds—the companies I've spoken to are delighted to permit it, provided they are debriefed on it so they can (a) learn something about what's not working in their own organizations themselves, and (b) learn about Customer Anthropology so they can do it with *their* customers.

The trick is introducing yourself to the people you'll be observing in a nonthreatening way, so they don't see you as a spy for their bosses. This requires being friendly and a bit self-deprecating—it doesn't hurt to portray yourself as a bit of a tourist and shrug about your assignment.

Your visit should not be a surprise—you need to ghostwrite an explanation of your visit for your customer's managers and have them send it to their employees before you arrive. It should say that your visit is to find out what *your* company can do to serve *them* better, to make their jobs easier, and not to evaluate or report on their performance.

Once you're in, you need to bring all the observational tools you can. Cameras, video and audio recorders, observation checklists—not all that different from birdwatchers' tools! You need to use them discreetly—turn off the flash, and make as little noise as you can. Find a "perch" where you can observe a lot without getting in people's way.

What you are looking for is anything that clearly does not work properly or effectively, such as:

- Workarounds: Things people do that the process, tools, and facilities obviously were not designed to accommodate, such as extra manual worksheets that are maintained because the computer reports don't do the job.
- User Torture: Evidence of obvious physical or psychological discomfort, such as people with phones cradled on their necks because they don't have headsets.
- Obstacles and Barriers: Signs that people can't do their jobs properly because something is physically or procedurally in their way, such as people who leave their stations for inordinately long times because they need to "get approvals."
- Repurposed Objects: Tools designed for one thing that have been appropriated for something else because no other suitable tool was available, such as makeshift doorstops to increase airflow or light in a factory.
- Wear Patterns: Evidence of stress or overuse, such as damaged power cords or hinges.

It's useful to observe competitors' customers as well, so you can see what your products' and services' relative strengths and weaknesses are and how they can be exploited.

As you observe, keep in mind the reason you are doing this: *Most organizations don't really know what's not working, or why.* There are many reasons for this.

It's usually easier and less hassle for employees to find workarounds than to complain to management and wait for them to act. Some of these workarounds circumvent management directives, so employees don't want management to know about them and won't admit to doing them. Also, most managers are out of touch with what really happens on the front lines of the organization, so there's no point asking them. Many employees don't even notice what doesn't work—they just get used to putting up with it or automatically finding workarounds, so there's no point asking them, either. Finally, surveys and interviews presuppose (often incorrectly) that you know how and why your customers are (and aren't) using your products and services.

Being an anthropologist takes a certain mind-set. You need to be patient—the devil is in the details, and it takes a while before you start to appreciate what is happening, and why, and start noticing things that you will miss initially. It takes concentration and focus and an ability to bring all your senses to bear (body language can convey a lot, for example) in your observation.

Going back and looking at/listening to your recordings can help you pick up things you missed the first time around, and letting other people watch/listen also can pick up what you miss. Watching someone do the same task twice, differently, or watching two people do the same task, differently, can be very informative.

Always keep in mind that things happen the way they do for a reason. The reason will not always be obvious, and you have to keep an open mind and not jump to conclusions about the reason. Interviewing people afterward to ask them why they think something is happening or is done a certain way can improve your perspective, but sometimes people just don't know. The anthropologist's job is to objectively record what is happening and figure out why.

What you will end up with is a list of things that are clearly not working properly or effectively and some validated hypotheses about why they aren't. Each of these is an opportunity (for you to do something with your product or service that will make it work better and fix what isn't working effectively), and a threat (if your competition's product or service beats you to it).

But beyond this, there is enormous value in Customer Anthropology in increasing your and your partners' understanding of your customers' businesses and industry, which can provoke all kinds of ideas for innovations, for new markets and product lines, and for expanding your presence with your customers to do more for them. This understanding also will improve your ability to strategize and improvise, reenergize your passion for what you do, and deepen your relationships with customers.

I've heard customer managers so impressed with the insight and understanding that came out of Customer Anthropology that they gave their observers the ultimate compliment: "In some ways it seems as if you now know our business better than we do." Now that's a powerful business tool!

Step 4b: Thinking the Customer Ahead Sessions

A generation ago, Nicholas Imparato and Oren Harari wrote a seminal book called *Jumping the Curve*[6] that introduces the concept of "thinking the customer ahead."

This is another way of addressing the problem that *people don't know what they need*. The idea of thinking the customer ahead is to engage in conversations with your most insightful and forward-thinking customers (and prospective customers)—your *pathfinders*—about what they *may* need in the future.

It's based on the concept of *scenarios*, alternative "pictures" of how the future of an industry or a segment of the population might evolve under various assumptions, and entails, after assessing these scenarios, asking the question: *What would that mean for our business, and our lives?* And then: *What would we need in that case that we don't need, or don't think we need, right now?*

This is, once again, an iterative, back-and-forth process. Your prospective customers need to assess the probability of various future scenarios and challenge and augment your assumptions. And then, with your prospective customers, you cocreate a picture of the future, detailed enough to identify needs.

Then you explore how those needs might be met, imagining possible solutions together.

Finally, you pull back to the present and assess the implications of these future needs for what your Natural Enterprise can do *now.*

Many great inventions got their start from someone imagining what might be needed, or possible, in the future, and then discovering that there was a market *immediately* for that idea. It's just that no one had ever thought of it before.

And as soon as people knew it was possible, they wondered how they ever did without it. Naturally, it had become a need.

Step 4c: Wisdom of Crowds Surveys

The Wisdom of Crowds concept is introduced in James Surowiecki's book of the same name,[7] and its thesis is essentially this:

> When they are asked appropriate questions, a reasonably informed, independent "crowd" of people will provide more reliable and accurate information than any number of "experts" asked the same questions.

In the context of identifying needs, the appropriate questions to ask a "crowd" might include:

- Predicting the success of a new product or service offering,
- Qualifying and ranking alternative ideas, products, processes, or technologies,
- Assessing the viability of a business decision,
- Deciphering the causes of a problem (if it's not too complex).

These tasks all entail making choices from a discrete range of alternatives. The "wisdom" comes from the fact that each member of a large and diverse crowd brings to the question some unique information that others (even experts) don't have, and that the judgment errors of such a large group tend to cancel each other out.

As an illustration, the median guess of a crowd guessing the number of jelly beans in a huge jar is almost invariably closer to the right number than the closest individual guess (and closer than the guesses of "expert" jelly-bean-counters).

The appropriate crowd in this case is your partners and prospective customers. Although generally speaking, surveys are not an effective way to gauge useful information about customer needs, if you have the opportunity to ask a very large number of people to rank their needs from a predetermined list, or to assess some ideas that could address those needs, you are likely to get a surprisingly accurate and reliable result.

And although your partners are unlikely to be numerous enough to constitute a "crowd," there is still strength in their number and diversity—when they clearly think that the idea that you are so passionate about is lame, *listen* to them.

A methodology for applying the Wisdom of Crowds technique is referenced in the resource guide. This technique also can be used to qualify ideas that emerge during the innovation process, so I'll have more to say about it in the next chapter.

Step 4d: Open Space Events

My friend Chris Corrigan is one of many leading-edge change facilitators who have been using a complex-situation problem-solving technique called Open Space events.[8] The critical differentiators between this technique and more traditional techniques for probing problems and possible solutions are:

- A high number of context-rich, small-group ideating and knowledge-sharing conversations;
- Attention to inviting and attracting the best possible people (Chris's colleague Michael Herman offers some wonderful

examples[9] of an invitation that would be hard for anyone who cares about the world to resist responding to);

- Participants self-select and self-manage;
- Passion (bounded by responsibility) is the fire that sparks and drives the energy and imagination of the session;
- The integral practice of being open to new ideas, new ways of thinking, and new ways of doing things, of suspending disbelief and skepticism, and of listening attentively; and,
- Freedom of each participant to decide what to do to act on the learning that comes from the session.

If you are looking for a way to find people to articulate their unmet needs and, at the same time, start to think about approaches to meeting them, I would recommend you consider Open Space. Facilitators for Open Space events are available at a very reasonable cost, and once you've been through the process once, you can start to employ Open Space techniques in all your research work.

Step 5: Make sense of it all

As a result of the first four steps in the research process, you are going to have an avalanche of information to try to digest. The process of doing so, called *sensemaking*, is more of an art than a science. It entails sitting down and wading through all that you have learned to date and asking yourselves: *What does it mean?*

There are a variety of sense-making methodologies that can help you with this. I think Barbara Minto's Structured Thinking or Pyramid Principle[10] process is an excellent one because it's rigorous and self-documenting. It requires you to create a pyramid that shows the information and data you have learned at the bottom, and the deductions and inferences you make based on that information in higher levels, until, at the top level, you have an hypothesis about an unmet need that your Natural Enterprise could address.

So if someone challenges your thinking on any particular point, you can point immediately to the underlying facts and information that support it and the process you used to deduce or infer your conclusion.

When you "read" the pyramid from top to bottom, it tells a *story* of what you've learned and how you've learned it, a very powerful way to establish the credibility of your argument and provide a context for your audience to understand it better.

Beyond this, the way in which you make sense of the information you have acquired in the previous research steps will depend on how you and your partners learn and collaborate. With practice, you'll learn to digest huge amounts of information, you'll hone your critical-thinking skills, and you'll become better collaborators. This is the very essence of Natural Enterprise, saying to each other: *Wow, that's interesting. What do we make of that? What opportunities does it suggest for us? Is there a need here that we might be able to fill?*

Step 6: The Needs Portfolio

Although the previous sense-making step entails digesting large amounts of information and thinking creatively about it, this next step is a more sober process, thinking critically and analytically about what the real opportunities are, and assembling a portfolio of Qualified Needs.

To do this you have to go back to the first step, think about your target customers, and begin to articulate a set of unmet needs for each customer segment, arising from the information and process you have followed in steps 2 though 5.

My clients have found the most effective way of articulating these needs is to express each need as a *story*. The story draws on the information that gave rise to the recognition of the need and is told from the perspective of a customer in the segment. Its purpose is to provide to you and your partners a rich context for understanding the need, which can be used in the process of innovating solutions to that need. (The innovation process is explained in the next chapter.)

So, for example, recall from our RST case study that the partners of this Natural Enterprise have agreed on this shared Purpose:

> Invent, develop, and deploy simple, inexpensive technologies that will reduce greenhouse gases, reduce oil dependency, and enable nations to become more self-sufficient.

Suppose the partners in RST have started to identify possible unmet needs for each of the customer segments they identified in step 1, and that for one segment, the "end consumers in affluent nations" segment, they have identified this candidate unmet need:

> Home lighting that runs on solar power, but can also switch to electric power when there hasn't been enough sunlight to keep the solar batteries charged.

Before putting this into the Needs Portfolio, they would do best to create a brief story that articulates this need. The story would explain how the as-yet-uninvented solution would work, and how and by whom it would be used. Would it draw on electricity automatically when the solar batteries ran low, perhaps using either a timer or a light-detector to determine whether light was actually needed? Would it be motion-sensor driven? Would it work only in places with a lot of sun, or could it be "programmed" for different sun regimens in different climates?

This critical, analytical activity is not about inventing solutions, it's about bringing clarity to *the job that is to be done* in order to meet the need.

For *each* customer segment or "constituency," then, the task in this step is to create a portfolio of unmet needs. Some of these needs may span several target customer segments; others may be unique to a single segment.

My clients have found two tools especially useful in this task—the need/affinity matrix, and the strategy canvas.

Step 6a: The Need/Affinity Matrix

To illustrate this matrix, I'm going to use the example of the plastic building materials (used for decking, fencing, playground equipment, etc.) industry, one that has emerged only in the last decade or so.

Some of the early players in this industry failed because they were too far ahead of the market, before the customer segments for products in this industry had really recognized a need for such products. Recently, thanks to a growing acceptance of plastics as durable and safer than some chemically treated woods, the market has been booming.

The task of creating the Needs Portfolio can be viewed as finding the intersections between "jobs to be done" (needs) and communities of people who do (or want to do) those "jobs" (affinities). This is illustrated in the need/affinity matrix below.

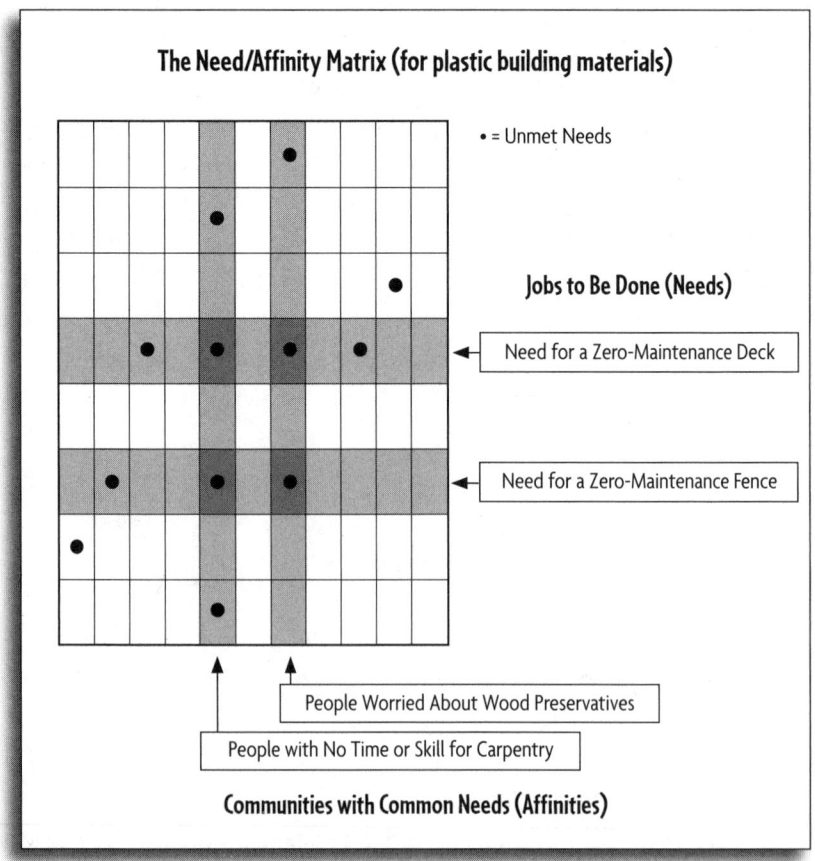

Note that this is not the way most designers and marketers ("the customer doesn't know what he wants") usually think or work. Designers think in terms of *features* and *benefits*. Customers think in terms of *the job to be done*. They don't want a ¼" drill bit (even if it plays MP3s); they want a ¼" *hole*. It's the jobs to be done that the Natural Entrepreneur should be looking for—jobs that existing products and services, for some reason, don't do satisfactorily. (And a reminder: Make sure you understand that reason—doing so can save you a lot of grief.)

Likewise, marketers generally think in terms of demographics ("twenty-one- to forty-nine-year-old white males"). But demographics are no longer the best way to parse your market: The days when a product could be made for a certain specific homogeneous age group, cultural group, or gender are long gone. Our *affinities*—the people or communities with whom we share a particular need or want—are now extremely complex, and getting more so.

So you need to find the intersections between (unmet) needs and affinities. In the example in the matrix above, vendors have recently (in the last decade or so) discovered an unmet customer need for decks and fences that require virtually no maintenance.

People don't have time to keep these structures looking beautiful. The solution the inventors came up with was molded plastic (or wood/plastic composite) decking—no cracks because of thermal resilience and no painting because the color is baked right in. The vendors discovered two main communities interested in such products—people with no time (or, if they were to be honest, lousy carpentry skills), and people worried about the newly discovered health and environmental dangers of creosote and other wood preservatives.

To use this tool, you list the needs (in terms of jobs to be done) down the side of the matrix, and the communities (in terms of their affinities) along the bottom. By marking off which affinity groups tend to need which jobs to be done, you find the "busiest intersections," which in this case are (a) people with no time or skill for carpentry and (b) people concerned about the chemicals in wood building materials, using building materials for (i) zero-maintenance decks and (ii) zero-maintenance fences. Four intersections in all, with significant populations of customers in them.

This defines both the need and the target market for companies producing plastic or composite decking/fencing products. It can help you define the need and target market for the products and services your Natural Enterprise proposes to offer, too.

Step 6b: The Strategy Canvas

A second need-identification tool is called a "strategy canvas" by its inventors, Kim and Mauborgne, in their book *Blue Ocean Strategy*.[11] The book, and the canvas, attempt to focus new product developers' attention on differentiation, what it is that makes your product or service dramatically different from that of your competitors' and, ideally, unique.

Consultant Kathy Sierra modified the canvas using the "equalizer" metaphor—the "sliders" you use for selecting how much bass versus

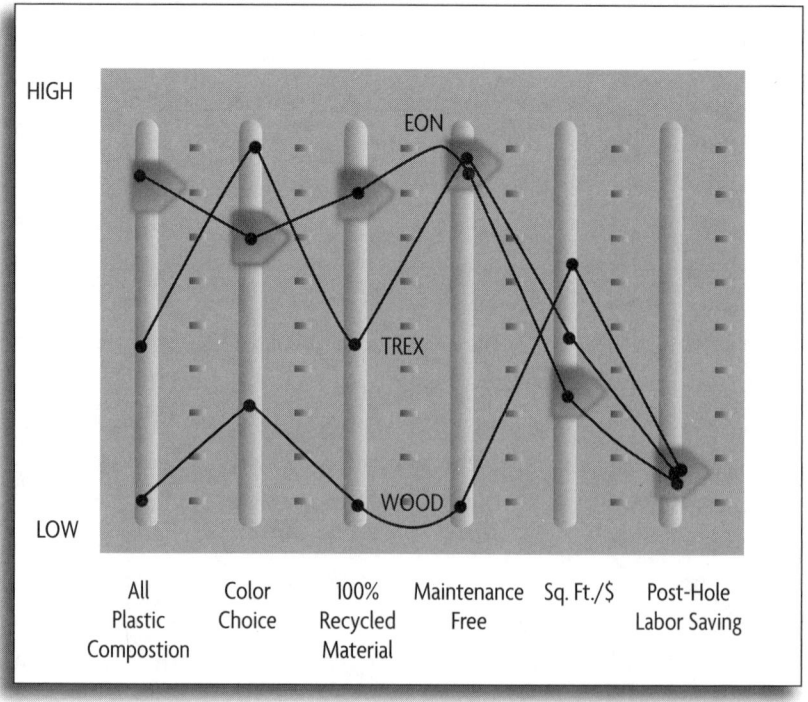

treble you want to hear through your speakers. The higher the slider is set, the better a product meets an attribute that customers care about. Sliders that are higher for your product than for your competitors' are competitive advantages in your industry; those that are lower are competitive weaknesses.[12]

The chart above shows how this canvas might look for Eon, a company that manufactures and distributes all-plastic decking, in contrast to two of its main competitors, Trex (a wood/plastic composite), and pressure-treated wood.

If the research behind this were correct, this would suggest that, in marketing, Eon should focus on the fact that it uses 100 percent recycled material and all-plastic composition that gives the product a high-tech look and feel. This canvas also suggests that the product's vulnerabilities are in color choice (where Trex has the advantage) and cost (where it is the most expensive of the three options). Disney theme parks, for example, selected Trex because, to them, maintenance-free qualities and color choice were paramount.

Although Eon and Trex are making great inroads into the decking market, they have not been as successful in the fencing market because one of the key customer-valued attributes of fencing is minimizing the labor of digging post holes, and the new products really aren't an improvement in that area. There's a great opportunity for an innovator who can come up with something that moves that sixth slider way up.

The inventors of plastic decking and fencing (back in the 1980s) didn't do very well, because people couldn't imagine using it. They couldn't visualize it. The iterators such as Eon and Trex who developed prototypes and installed a few free of charge so that customers and neighbors could see what they were getting, kick the tires, and suggest improvements—those were the vendors who made money filling this need.

The horizontal axis of the need/affinity matrix was also initially fuzzy. With less time available each year, customers clearly were clamoring for lower-maintenance products. But those customers probably would be loath to admit that, compared to previous generations, they just didn't have the skills to build, repair, or maintain such structures.

And who would have guessed, if they hadn't done a lot of research "in the crowd," that consumer concerns about health, safety, and the environment would lead to an aversion to, and then a ban on, creosote and other toxic wood preservatives, throwing the entire industry open to new competitors?

And what about people in struggling nations who don't have electricity? Snap-together decking does away with the need for power tools.

Research entails interviewing and surveying as many people as possible to get a consensus on not only the need but also the categories of customer, the affinity groups, who have that need. Such primary research would ask questions on issues such as:

- The aesthetic acceptability of various styles, colors, and options of plastic decking and fencing;
- How the relative noisiness of a plastic deck (due to its lower sound-deadening qualities) and "cracking" noises during thermal expansion and contraction in the sun, affects its attractiveness;
- To what extent the light weight of a plastic fence detracts from the sense of security it offers;
- The willingness of home centers to make room to stock and support a product that competes with its wood products; and,
- The willingness of contractors to pass along the savings from faster installation to their customers (do they see this as a threat of fewer hours, or an opportunity for higher margins?), and so forth.

This is hard work, but as long as you have the time and passion for it, it's not expensive. It will give you a lot of information about the communities of customers who will buy your product or service, and, by iteration, exactly what they would prefer to buy. That puts you light-years ahead of traditional companies, who invent in a lab, design in a vacuum, and then advertise to anyone who will listen and hope for the best.

So the partners of RST would position the perceived need for switchable solar/electric home lighting products as one of the rows on *their* need/affinity matrix, and mark the customer segments they identified as needing such products in the corresponding columns.

And then on the strategy canvas for this type of product, they'd identify the buying criteria of the applicable customer segments for such products along the horizontal axis, and rate their "ideal" not-yet-invented product against existing products on each of these buying criteria, to assess whether the need appeared to be large enough that a product, appropriately differentiated according to these criteria, would be successful in the marketplace.

This, of course, requires a deep knowledge of customers' needs, affinities, and buying criteria—one that can be achieved only by painstaking and thorough research, both primary and secondary.

So at the end of this step you have a list of potential needs, with a story for each one, positioned on your need/affinity matrix and strategy canvas.

The next step is to find out why someone else hasn't filled this need already.

Step 7: Assess why the need isn't already met

Now you have to return to primary and secondary research to try to discover why the need you have identified isn't already met by some product or service on the market. This is a critical step: There is *always* a reason. The market isn't perfect, but there are enough people and companies on a constant lookout for market opportunities that if it was as simple as designing and marketing a product from today's technology, someone is more than likely to have done it already.

> Now you have to discover why the need you have identified isn't already met by some product or service on the market. This is a critical step. *There is always a reason.*

There are a number of reasons why unmet needs may not yet have been exploited by anyone.

For example, the technology needed to meet the need may need further work, or may exist only in another application whose applicability to this particular need has not been recognized, or in nature its applicability to this particular need has not yet been discovered, like the applicability of the zero-pigment coloring of butterfly wings to the thin-film coatings industry, as described in the introduction to this book.

Or, the major players in the market may see the particular need as too small for their large scale, so that it is perceived as only a "niche product" opportunity.

The perceived solutions to this unmet need also may be seen as unaffordable by the identified customer segments. Many pharmaceutical and health products to treat diseases that are only endemic to struggling nations fall in this category.

Or, the solution may be too complicated. Hundreds of products that meet needs perfectly well have failed because it was just too difficult for the customers to understand how to use them. More than half of all returns of electronic products today, a recent study showed, were not because of product defects but because the customers just couldn't figure out how to use them properly.

Other reasons may be that the customer segments have not yet realized they have such a need. The plastic decking example described above was in this category for a decade, to the dismay of its early inventors, who were simply too far ahead of the market. Or, the customer market may be too thin or undefined. If there are a million potential customers worldwide for a product, but they are spread across the globe and lack any affinity for telling each other about the product, so that it is impossible to reach even a significant subset of them through a targeted awareness campaign, it is unlikely that most of the potential customers for the product even know the product exists.

Whatever the reason *may* be, don't give up until you know why the need you've identified hasn't already been met. Gather some intelligence from potential competitors to discover why they've not acted on it. Talk to your pathfinders to discover what happened when they tried to find a solution to the need. Talk to marketing people, designers, inventors, and technology experts to get their take on it.

When you find the reason, one of two things will happen: Either you'll realize that you're not going to be able to get around this reason (in which case you should delete it from your portfolio and perhaps revisit the idea at a future time when the situation may have changed) or you'll decide you can find a solution that gets around the reason others haven't entered this market. In the latter case, it now becomes a Qualified Need, and you're ready to move it forward to the next step.

Step 8: Assess how the need fits with your competencies and resources

The last hurdle for the Qualified Needs in your portfolio is to assess whether you and your partners have the competencies (the knowledge, Gifts, and the twelve capacities outlined in the introduction, to the extent they apply) and have or can obtain the resources (technical, human, and financial) to bring this unmet need to commercial viability.

If a Qualified Need has made it this far in the process, it is likely that you should be able to conclude that you do have the competencies and do have (or can get) the resources you need to commercialize it. It is only if you are really sure that you're just biting off far more than you can chew that you should abandon a Qualified Need at this last hurdle. Nevertheless, it's worth talking about with your partners. If you can do it, but it's going to put you head-to-head with Microsoft or Google in the not-too-distant future, you might want to think carefully before proceeding.

If you've followed this process, you should now have a portfolio of unmet needs, qualified so you know (a) why these needs aren't already being met in the marketplace, (b) that your Natural Enterprise has the competencies and resources to deliver on these needs, and (c) that doing so will allow each of you to exercise your Gifts and Passions and achieve your shared Purpose.

The next challenge is imagining product and service ideas that will meet those needs and bringing them to fruition. That's the subject of the next chapter.

CHAPTER 3 CASE STUDY
Finding a need to fill in the local community

Tall Grass Prairie Bread Company

Winnipeg, Manitoba, is a Canadian city with a fierce entrepreneurial and independent spirit. Its citizens are so cosmopolitan, informed, and particular that the city is often used as a test market for innovations.

The Tall Grass Prairie Bread Company is a Natural Enterprise in Winnipeg that grew out of a natural community—the ecumenical church that its founders belonged to. The church included people from various religious backgrounds with a strong sense of community and an avowed shared Purpose—to do something collaboratively to make the community a better place.

The first thing they decided to do was to "adopt" a local grain-farming family that was struggling because of low grain prices. They bought grains from the farm at fair prices, and created a co-op in the church kitchen that baked bread. Co-op members distributed the bread throughout the community, and bought and sold it at cost.

Their success caused several of them to expand the co-op and establish a bakery that could help support more farmers and employ more people in the community. Here's what they do that's different:

- As a matter of principle, they buy only from farmers who use natural growing techniques—no artificial fertilizers or pesticides—and who steward their land responsibly. Their products are certified 100 percent organic.

- When the local bank laughed at their business model, they borrowed from customers and community members, with no promise of repayment—they would repay if and when they could.
- The farmers deliver their grain direct to the bakery and sit and meet with the customers. The customers learn where their food comes from, its *story,* and become rabidly faithful.
- When the bakery was wildly more popular than they expected, or were ready to deal with, they didn't panic—they improvised.
- They pay both farmers and staff generously (by competitive standards) and still make enough to sustain themselves, and to innovate into new products.
- They buy from suppliers who share their ethical operating principles, and those suppliers return their kindness.
- Operating principles include a two-hundred-mile rule—supplies travel only about two-hundred miles (one-tenth the distance competitors' supplies travel)—which gives them resilience against transportation cost increases.

They strive for continuous innovation, continuous improvement. "The questions that we continue to ask," cofounder Tabitha Langel says, "are how can we be *more* local, *more* just, *more* environmentally conscious than we were yesterday." Better, not bigger.

– 4 –

IMAGINING AND INNOVATING SOLUTIONS
offering something significantly different

Logic will get you from A to B. Imagination is everything. It will take you everywhere. It is the preview of life's coming attractions.

—Albert Einstein

You can never change things by fighting the existing reality. To change something, build a new model that makes the existing model obsolete.

—Buckminster Fuller

Just as energy is the basis for life itself, and ideas the source of innovation, so is innovation the vital spark of all human change, improvement and progress.

—Ted Levitt, HBR[1]

The last chapter explained the process of research to identify unmet needs. This chapter will describe the practice of imagining possibilities and gathering ideas that might address those needs, and the process of innovation, which converts those ideas into your Natural Enterprise's offerings—products and services. It is through this process that needs are transformed into ideas and ideas in turn are "realized," made real.

This chapter also will explain the six guiding principles of innovation and the land mines that successful innovators must learn to avoid. Finally, it will explain the concept of disruptive innovation and how such innovation provides Natural Entrepreneurs with a powerful competitive advantage relative to large "industrial" corporations.

The practice of imagining

I included imagination skills in the list of twelve essential capacities in the introduction to this book, because they are skills that not many people possess. Although they can be learned, some of us are just naturally better at imagining than others. Our education system tends to discourage imagination, driving it out of many of us. Many large organizations also make no room for imagination, and those who possess it either sublimate it or choose to leave those organizations.

As a result, business and our economy now suffer from a tragic imaginative poverty. Consumer demand no longer comes from imaginative new offerings that tap unmet needs; instead, this demand is "manufactured" by intensive, manipulative advertising, promotion, and marketing campaigns. Yet if you look at the most profound, groundbreaking new products in our society—the foods of the Green Revolution, new fabrics in our clothes, amazing new materials and products used in constructing our homes and offices, new technologies that have transformed the information and

> The most profound, groundbreaking new products in our society are all the result of great imagination focused on trying to address deep human needs.

entertainment industries—they are all the result of great imagination focused on trying to address deep human needs.

Imagination skills can be relearned, but there is no imagination "process." Rather, imagining is a practice, a competency that you acquire by just doing it.

In practicing this myself, and in studying some of the imaginative entrepreneurs I have met during many years as an advisor to them, I have learned several important things about imagining.

First, imagination is almost always driven by a need—a problem, a blockage, a dissatisfaction, or a need for self-expression. Even children playing made-up games are challenging themselves to overcome obstacles, difficulties, to learn how to do something better. Second, imagination requires suspension of disbelief and conjuring something up out of nothing. Although the focus on a need keeps imagination anchored and directed, thinking of imaginative ideas and solutions must be free of all preconceptions and awareness of practical restrictions. It is the job of the *innovator* to make the imagined idea real (we'll talk about that process soon); the job of the *imaginer*, by contrast, is to conceive of something radically new, unbounded by knowledge of what exists now, inventing something that no one has thought of before.

I've also learned that imagination is sparked by inspirations from nature and by ideas from other disciplines and areas of human activity. It has been said there is nothing new under the sun. If you look at the great inventions of history, they were almost all provoked or inspired by discoveries, learning, and appreciation of ideas from elsewhere, applied analogously to the need at hand. The carburator used in modern engines, for example, drew its inspiration from an analogous process used in ancient aqueducts.

And, finally, I've found that ideas—*the results of imagination*—are best conveyed through stories. In order for ideas to be appreciated by those other than the imaginer, they must be translated, put into a context that others can grasp. This is really what art is about, as all forms of art (not just literature) are

> **Ideas–the results of imagination–are best conveyed through stories.**

essentially stories that contextualize what the artist has imagined.

Here's a story to give you some appreciation of how imagination is almost always driven by a need.

I'm a birdwatcher, and I have tried several inventions to try to dissuade squirrels from stealing all the birdseed I put out before the birds can get to it. Yesterday, while I watched, two squirrels were looking at a new bird feeder I'd bought, equipped with a "squirrel baffle," a device that looks like a musical cymbal designed to block animals trying to climb up the feeder pole, and a spring device on the bird feeder perches that closes the feeder openings when something heavier than a bird rests on them.

These two devices—the baffle and the spring closure—were imaginative ideas that addressed an unmet need (preventing squirrels from hogging all the seed meant for the birds), ideas that were then converted, through the process of innovation, into products that "realized" the idea and met the need.

How did the squirrels respond when facing this innovation, *which created a new need for them*—to find a way to get the seeds by circumventing the baffle and not tripping the spring closure?

As I observed this pair of squirrels, this is what I saw; the entire process took about an hour:

- They tried the old way, climbing up the pole, using various methods to get around the baffle from the bottom, unsuccessfully.
- They observed the birds, which were unaffected by the baffle.
- They tried to leap to the bird feeder from a nearby tree branch, above the baffle, unsuccessfully.
- They took a running leap from a distance, landed on top of the sloped baffle, and promptly slipped off back to the ground.
- They took a running leap from a distance, landed on top of the sloped baffle, and immediately wrapped their forepaws around the pole just above the baffle; they then climbed up to the feeder unimpeded, but were defeated by the spring closure, which closed the feeder opening as soon as they put one paw on it.
- They took a running leap from a distance, landed on top of the sloped baffle, and immediately wrapped their forepaws around the pole just above the baffle; they then climbed up to the very top of the pole above the feeder, and hung from the feeder pole upside down by their hind paws and scooped the seed out of the feeder opening with their forepaws without tripping the spring closure. Five minutes later, the feeder was empty.

What was interesting was that it took both squirrels to accomplish this feat: The first one mastered the baffle leap, and the second one figured out the upside-down hang. Together they made a remarkable Natural Enterprise, with combined Gifts and a shared Passion for their collective Purpose!

What they exhibited was not creativity or innovation, but imagination—there is a difference.

> **Creativity** is the ability to model things concretely in the real world. It is the capacity to convert an idea or representation into a product or service, something tangible. *Innovation* is the process of exercising that capacity in a systematic and disciplined way.
>
> **Imagination** is an ability to conceptualize something out of nothing. It is the capacity to draw on information and to conceive of possibilities that convert that information into an idea.

Studies of animals have shown enormous variability in imagination in any one species. It is quite possible that two different squirrels might never have figured out how to conquer the human innovations to access the birdseed. I think it is likely that neither of the squirrels in my yard would have succeeded alone.

It is clear that they used experimentation to add to their available information, but their discovery of the means to defeat the baffle and the spring closure was not just dumb trial and error. They thought about it and *imagined* the ways to succeed before they tried them out.

The resource guide at the end of this book suggests some ways to practice imagination, by opening oneself to new possibilities, being "present" in the moment and focusing on the need, paying attention, letting go of preconceptions and judgments about what might be practical, reflecting, and letting ideas just come to you, emerge in your consciousness. This might sound mystical but any artist, fiction writer, or inventor will tell you it is a learned practice, and it is even something that groups of people who are all skilled at the practice can do collaboratively.

Janine Benyus[2] has written a marvelous book on how to allow your imagination to be sparked by inspirations from nature. It is called *Biomimicry*, which she describes as:

> a new science that studies nature's models and then imitates or takes inspiration from these designs and processes to solve human problems; a new way of viewing and valuing nature that introduces an era based not on what we can extract from the natural world, but on what we can learn from it— what nature has learned after 3.8 billion years of evolution: what works, what lasts.

The example I gave in the introduction to illustrate my Gift, the idea of applying an understanding of the ways butterfly wings achieve color through light refraction rather than pigment, to prevent counterfeiting of banknotes and to "paint" airplane wings, is a perfect example of biomimicry.

Other examples she proffers include ceramics based on how abalone make their shells, glues based on the secretions of mussels, and solar-cell technologies based on how leaves capture solar energy and how microbes store it. Her Biomimicry Institute offers courses in learning from nature.

This is something we do instinctively—it's how we learned before formal education was developed. It's about paying attention to what nature has been doing for millennia and thinking imaginatively about applications of these natural "technologies" to human needs and problems.

Or conversely, it's about thinking by analogy, starting with a problem or need and asking "How would nature solve this problem?" or, more likely, "How *has* nature solved this problem?"

Once you have a collection of ideas that might address the needs you are focused on, you need to learn to convey them in the form of stories. The resource guide at the

> Start with a problem or need and ask, "How would nature solve (or how has it already solved) this problem?"

end of the book provides some books and articles that will hone your story-crafting and storytelling skills.

Storytelling is another skill that takes a lot of practice. It's a performance art that, like all performances, requires crafting a compelling text, rehearsal, conveyance of energy and passion, and clarity of exposition and delivery. But it's a skill worth acquiring and practicing. Like imagining, it's an essential skill in every Natural Enterprise.

Imagining is the first step in the innovation process, which I'll describe in a moment. First, however, I want to explain the six guiding principles of innovation.

The guiding principles of innovation

Innovation is *the process of taking ideas and putting them to practical use*, figuring out how they might work in the real world.

The most innovative organizations I've worked with have taught me that this process cannot be followed mechanically—it must be guided by an understanding of the principles that govern good innovation practices, that determine why some innovations are successful and others are not, and that appreciate why people are often reluctant to embrace even brilliant innovations.

Here are the six guiding principles of innovation that I've learned from my practice as an innovation consultant:

1. *Innovation is usually prompted by passion and good intentions:* Innovation has always been about improving the quality of human life (although some of the resulting technologies have had some disastrous unintended consequences). Because innovation takes perseverance and often entails considerable risk, innovators usually have a passion to make things better. If you can tap into that passion in your partners, your pathfinder customers, and others, the innovations that result will likely be much better than if you outsource some innovation work, or try to buy it, or bring in outside "experts" to make it happen.

2. *Most people accept innovations reluctantly:* People change much more slowly than technology, and ultimately won't accept, adopt, or pay for any technology that they aren't yet ready for, or that doesn't fill a real human need. Innovations that don't meet such needs are called fads, and they rarely last. If the need is not yet well recognized (you're ahead of the market), your innovations had better at least be easy and fun to adopt.

3. *Innovation is driven by need and fueled by imagination:* If either need or imagination is lacking, your innovations are likely to be sterile, incremental, and disconnected from prospective customers—and not very successful.

4. *Innovation starts with the customer:* If all your research has been secondary (reading and online) rather than primary (face-to-face with prospective customers), you're probably going to come up with innovations that customers don't need (or don't know they need) and don't want. And the innovation process itself has to be customer-facing, to the extent that your customers (at least your pathfinders) are your innovation partners, codeveloping your new offerings with you.

5. *Customers often don't know what innovations they need:* This may sound as though it contradicts principle number 4, but it doesn't. It's when you observe and know the customer so well, and the customer knows your capability well, and you work together to identify the customer's unmet needs (even before they have articulated them) that you can start, together, identifying the ideas and innovations that can meet those needs.

6. *Innovations, like ideas, are discovered as often as they are invented:* Nature is a brilliant innovator, as well as a great source of ideas. And as the TV series *Connections*[3] demonstrated, many of the world's most brilliant innovations were transplanted from one area of application or discipline to another by an observant, creative mind. Pay attention, think analogously, and cast a wide net in your environmental scan and readings, and you'll probably find the innovation that realizes the idea that transforms the need is already out there, uncommercialized, just waiting for you to discover.

Now that you have some context for how to use it, here is the "best practices" innovation process that I have been using with my clients in recent years. It is gleaned from more than two decades of working with more than a hundred entrepreneurial organizations and learning which innovation programs, practices, and techniques work, and which ones don't. I've distilled it down to six essential steps.

The innovation process

Let's return to our RST case study. In the last chapter, we identified that, in order to achieve its collective Purpose, which was to

> invent, develop, and deploy simple, inexpensive technologies that will reduce greenhouse gases, reduce oil dependency, and enable nations to become more self-sufficient,

RST had, in conducting its research, agreed on the following unmet need:

> Home lighting that runs on solar power, but can also switch to electric power when there hasn't been enough sunlight to keep the solar batteries charged.

Suppose that, for this need, and each of the others in the Needs Portfolio they have identified, they have crafted a story to envisage how a solution to the need might ideally work. Each need in the Needs Portfolio has then been mapped by potential customer category on RST's need/affinity matrix, and for each customer segment a strategy canvas has been created, showing the strengths and weaknesses of existing products in meeting these needs.

We're now going to take one sample unmet need—the switchable solar/electric home lighting need that RST identified for its "end consumers in affluent nations" customer segment, through the six steps of the innovation process illustrated below.

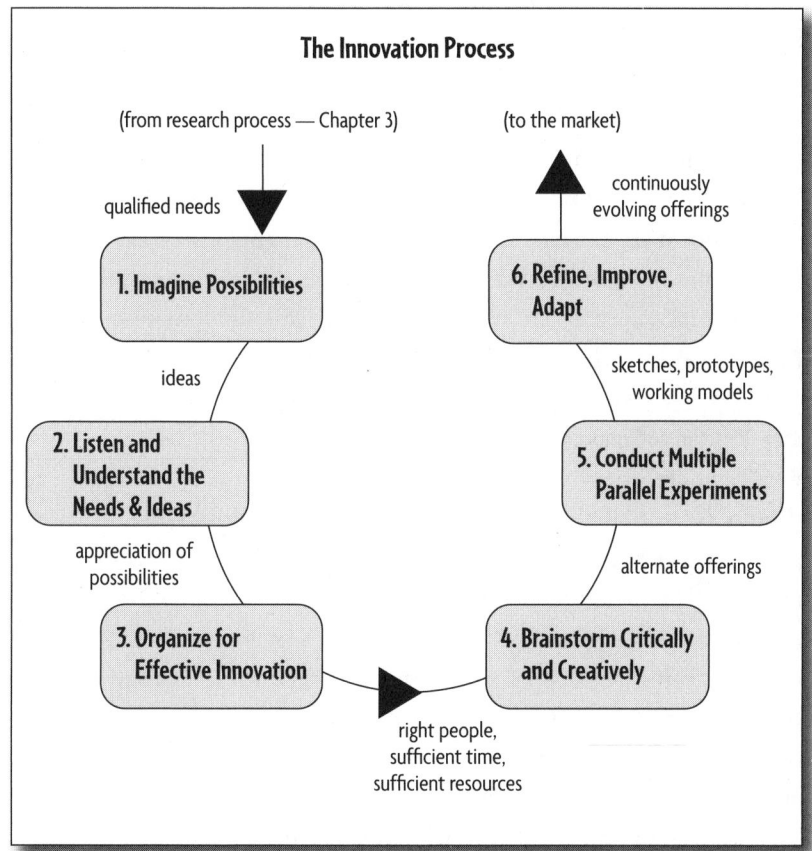

Step 1: Imagine possibilities

The practice of imagining possibilities, transforming needs into ideas that might meet those needs, was described earlier in this chapter. The partners of RST would, working individually and collectively, take each of the needs in the Needs Portfolio that emerged from their research and imagine a set of possible ideas for it.

So, for example, they might imagine a lightbulb with a solar collector, a solar battery, a light-detector, and a switch that would automatically deploy when it is dark and the solar battery is low.

As alternatives, they might imagine a similar lightbulb that would deploy only when a built-in motion sensor was tripped. Or they might imagine a centralized solution where the solar collectors, solar batteries, and switch were on the roof, and would switch all the lightbulbs in the house from solar to electric power when it was dark and when the central bank of solar batteries was low.

Perhaps Janis, as the engineer in the enterprise, would propose a biomimicry solution—copying and adapting the night-lighting "technology" used by fireflies to light up the dark using biofuels.

The point at this stage is to get as many ideas brought to the surface as possible, and not discard or critique ideas or rush to solutions.

The outcome of this stage is an Ideas Portfolio mapped to the Needs Portfolio that came out of the research process.

Step 2: Listen and understand the needs and ideas

The next step begins by convening an Innovation Team. This team should consist of the partners in your Natural Enterprise, selected pathfinder customers identified in the research process, and any other individuals who can be invited to explore the ideas, and who have passion for the subject. In the case of RST's switchable solar/electric home lighting ideas, this might include renewable energy associations, government departments responsible for energy and the environment, public foundations, universities interested in the research, and perhaps even possible investors.

The entire Team then gets briefed with the stories that have been developed to support each of the needs and an explanation of each of the ideas in the Ideas Portfolio pertinent to that need. A Q&A session would follow to get each of the Team members up to speed. A selected Team member (or possibly an outside facilitator) would then explain the rest of the innovation process, so that everyone understands the work ahead.

It is possible that, as a result of the discussion at this stage, more information may be required. Someone on the team would be assigned to gather the information, either through primary (interview, survey) or secondary (reading, online) research, and convey it to the rest of the team. Before proceeding to the next step, it is important that all Team members have a full understanding of the needs and ideas, and an appreciation of the possibilities the ideas present.

Step 3: Organize for effective innovation

This step is principally about creating time and space for the steps that follow, and providing the necessary resources (such as money for prototypes, fees for outside experts, parts, and supplies) for these steps.

This step may seem obvious, but it is the one that, in my experience, is most prone to failure, and failure to do it properly is the most common cause of an unsuccessful innovation process. I have seen some brilliant ideas ripe for great disruptive innovation abandoned because there was some technical issue or missing information that no one was able to deal with, or assigned to deal with. I also have seen organizations, large and small, abandon very promising ideas because something came up related to day-to-day operations, or the personal lives of the partners, and there just wasn't time to pursue them.

Innovation is far more about hard work than imagination and creativity. Some of that work is tedious, unglamorous, and time-consuming. You need to organize to make sure someone is given the time and responsibility to do it. And you need to create the space, away from the daily business and personal routines of your partners and others on the Innovation Team, to ensure that each idea gets proper consideration, to ensure that good, difficult ideas aren't abandoned in favor of incremental, easy ideas, and to ensure that enough concentrated effort is applied to each idea, by the right people, to give it a fair, creative, and critical airing and to carry it through to fruition.

Step 4: Brainstorm critically and creatively

Brainstorming is both art and science, and it works best when the participants like and trust each other, and bring diverse points of view, knowledge, and capacities to the process. It is often best when it is a facilitated process, where the facilitator explains the process carefully at the outset, documents the thoughts and decisions that emerge, and referees the process to ensure that disagreements don't sidetrack the process, that decisions are made knowledgeably, and that ideas are neither abandoned too early (the best ideas are often the most challenging, but worth it) nor allowed to outlive their usefulness (which often happens when you get one person who crusades relentlessly for it, to the point that others give up trying to argue).

One advantage of Natural Enterprises over traditional hierarchical corporations is that it is harder for a more "senior" person to adopt a pet project and use his or her clout and position to push it ahead of better but "unsponsored" projects.

There is a bit of "yin and yang" to the brainstorming process. On one hand, you want critical thinking, because you don't want to invest a lot of time, energy, and resources in an idea that is fatally flawed. On the other hand, you want creative people who will respond to criticisms with workarounds that keep the idea in play. In good brainstorming sessions you hear a lot of "what if," "yes, but ..." and "yes, and ..." conversations.

> **Brainstorming is essentially a conversation, and should be conducted as such—politely, everyone taking turns, everyone listening before they assess, and thinking before they speak.**

Brainstorming is essentially a conversation, and should be conducted as such—politely, everyone taking turns, everyone listening before they assess, and thinking before they speak, no one dominating, no one keeping quiet about some nagging doubt and then saying later "I thought this would be a problem," and no one being a wallflower.

Brainstorming sessions need to be documented: For each idea, the facilitator should be keeping track, ideally on a large board or (if you're skilled at using this technology) a mindmap, visible to everyone throughout the session, what the advantages and weaknesses of each idea were, what additional information is needed before moving forward with it (and who will get that information, and how), and the conclusion (go forward with the idea, abandon it, park it until additional information is available, shelve it as an idea too far ahead of its time) reached by consensus. Ideally, for each need in the Needs Portfolio, you want to advance at least two significantly different offering ideas that could address it, but not too many different offering ideas (or else you'll spread your resources to follow up on them too thin).

Your "output" from this step is a set of a few Alternate Offerings for each need in the Needs Portfolio and the documentation supporting each of these alternatives.

The resource guide at the end of the book provides links to some excellent articles and books about brainstorming, and about the art of conversation.

In our RST example, we might imagine that the "firefly" biomimicry idea for switchable solar/electric home lighting might be besieged early as too radical. The Innovation Team should have enough people with diverse knowledge and perspectives to assess whether it is an idea that just needs some good research with a qualified research partner to bring forward; an idea that is just too far ahead of its time to warrant resources now (and therefore "parked" for later rethinking, rather than abandoned); or an impractical idea that should be put to rest.

We also might imagine that two clearly different ideas would emerge that would get forwarded as Alternate Offerings, one a decentralized solution (which would work in an individual light socket), and another a centralized solution (where all lights would be switched at once by a central sensing and switching setup).

And perhaps the brainstorming might produce some additional Alternate Offerings that never surfaced during step 1, such as a Directed Light that, rather than casting the LCD luminescence equally in all directions, allowed it to be focused, with some intuitive pointing device, on the book, the hands, the computer, or whatever other device specifically needed light. Or even, for conservationists, a romantic setting that, until overridden, simulated the light from a candle instead of the light from a normal lightbulb.

Step 5: Conduct multiple parallel experiments

The reason you want several significantly different Alternate Offerings for each need in your Needs Portfolio is that, if you have only one offering to test and commercialize, you will be wedded to that offering and unwilling to abandon it even if it's hopeless.

You should conduct experiments of various types (depending on the nature of the offering) on each alternative. Those experiments could include:

- Build prototypes using different supplies and methods. Develop lots of different sketches[4] that cost little or nothing to produce and let different people kick them around—users, designers, parts suppliers, and so on.

- Simulate how each alternative would work, ideally using inexpensive materials—you're just trying to give everyone a real sense of how the alternative would be used, how well it meets the unmet need, not jumping, yet, to exactly how it would be designed or look.

- When simulations aren't applicable, craft stories of how each alternative would work, stories with a real script about how a customer of RST, for example, would use the switchable home lighting when they came home at the end of the day and on the weekend, when lighting might be needed for longer periods. Expose these stories to customers and probe their responses—would they use it? (Remember, people are reluctant to change their buying behavior until they have no choice.) How much would they pay? Where would they buy it?

- Talk early to suppliers (of both labor and materials) to see what would be available if you decided to commercialize each alternative. If they see a big market, this will give them time to do some innovation of their own and come up with an economic way to supply just what you need—even if it doesn't exist yet.

- Don't lose track of what competitors may be doing while you've been innovating. They may have ideas you can take from, or you may even find it makes sense to partner with them.

- Ask yourself, every step of the way, *Is this offering sufficiently different from what anyone else is offering?* To succeed as a Natural Enterprise, you must fill an *unmet* need.

- Assess whether it's a good "fit" for your Natural Enterprise. Is it still "on Purpose" for you, or have you compromised your Purpose and principles

> Ask yourself, every step of the way, "Is this offering sufficiently different from what anyone else is offering?"

for an idea that just looks very profitable? Does it fit with your and your partners' Gifts and Passions? Is this something you really want to do, consistent with your values?
- Recall what you discovered during your research about why no other company was already filling that need. Do your alternatives get around the obstacles that kept others out of this market? Have those obstacles changed or gone away?
- Consider whether you have the resources to provide each alternative on a commercial scale. For some items, one-offs may be economical (especially if you're meeting a local unmet need, where buyers will favor you over competitors from outside your community). For others, you may need considerable money, materials, processing capacity, and talent to produce an economical quantity of the offering. Can you buy, hire, or otherwise get these resources? Can you partner with someone who will bring them in at their cost?

The key to multiple parallel experiments is to "fail early and inexpensively." Every experiment and every failure is a learning experience that will help you make your offerings more successful and valuable.

Even at this stage, you need not narrow your choice down to a single alternate offering for each need in your Needs Portfolio. You can take more than one alternative to market, where you may discover there are different markets for each.

Step 6: Refine, improve, adapt

Many books have been written about "continuous improvement," and I'll talk more about *continuous improvisation* in the final chapter of this book. How you go about commercializing your offerings depends on the nature of those offerings, and is beyond the scope of this book. What's important is that, to the extent your customers and suppliers will accommodate it, you never stop tinkering, listening, gauging the market, responding to what's new and what's needed and what might be a little bit better.

The land mines of innovation

The clients of mine whose businesses failed did so for one predominant reason: *Their supposedly innovative offerings failed to fill an unmet need*, so they ended up trying to differentiate themselves by advertising, branding, marketing, or other cosmetic means.

There are eight land mines of innovation, traps you can fall into when you think you're being innovative, but you really aren't. They are:

> **Insufficient differentiation:** I've known many entrepreneurs who either failed to do their research (and didn't find out until it was too late that there were already competitors in the "market space" they tried to occupy), or so admired some successful business that they thought they'd copy the model and tweak it a bit to make it different (open in a different location or offer products and services that differed only in ways customers didn't care about). Learn the sad lesson of so many franchisees: In business, imitation can be fatal.
>
> **Not understanding why a niche exists:** Too many entrepreneurs fail to appreciate that, although the market is far from perfect, there are usually good business reasons that what appears to be an untapped niche market is probably no market at all. Make sure you know *why* the unmet need you've identified isn't already being met by established players in the industry.
>
> **Being too far ahead of or behind the market:** I've met several entrepreneurs who were so enamored of their inventions that they couldn't believe everyone else wouldn't love them as much as they did. Some of them lost their life savings as a result.

Make sure your prospective customers "get" the value of your proposed product or service and are prepared to pay for it and to be evangelists for it. Be alert, too, for the possibility that, when you describe it to them, they may tell you what they think you want to hear instead of the truth.

Growth dependency: Too many businesses become absolutely dependent on growth to remain viable. They need the extra cash from operations each year to finance the extra costs they incurred the previous year, in an endless struggle to achieve viable margins and volume for products and services that are commodities, always under price pressure from competitors' look-alikes. Make sure your prospective offerings are sufficiently innovative and unique that your enterprise is viable and sustainable *without* growth, and agile enough to adapt even if the economy sours, or if you get tied up in costly litigation, or if some other crisis occurs.

Offering a solution in search of a problem: A lot of entrepreneurs are inventors, scientists, artists, artisans, administrators, teachers, or managers. Sales is not their forte, and they're more comfortable working with ideas, materials, plans, or systems than with those pesky people called customers. If you're not comfortable spending a lot of face time with customers, you have to partner with someone who is. Some new products out there are quite intriguing, but because they don't meet a real, unmet customer need, they'll never be more than that.

> If you're not comfortable spending a lot of face time with customers, you have to partner with someone who is.

Groupthink: It's natural, when you start kicking around ideas you're passionate about with people you love, to get caught up in the enthusiasm and not consider the problems or challenge the assumptions and information being bandied around. Make sure there is sufficient diversity, knowledge, and critical thinking in your enterprise to ensure that unwarranted optimism and dubious assumptions and forecasts are challenged.

Unaffordable Offerings: Entrepreneurs often underestimate the amount of work that needs to be done to commercialize a product or service offering successfully. If you're beholden to outside investors or lenders, that may cause you to price your product at a level that your customers, as much as they need and want it, cannot afford or cannot justify paying. Or it can cause you to price the offering below your cost of production, so that your enterprise runs out of cash and becomes insolvent and unable to continue operating.

Unfeasible Offerings: The innovation process is by nature idealistic. You're imagining what's possible, and then doing all you can to realize that imagined ideal. Inherently, this can result in offerings that are technically unfeasible (the science, technology, materials, or other supplies just aren't at the stage yet where they can be commercialized).

Disruptive innovation: The Natural Entrepreneur's competitive advantage

The third and final part of this book explains how the culture of Natural Enterprises tends to differ dramatically from that of traditional corporations. Much of this cultural difference stems from the fact that Natural Enterprises are flat, nonhierarchical, independent cooperative organizations with a shared Purpose, complementary Gifts and Passions, uncommon core capacities, and a shared vision.

Most large corporations are anything but innovative. Because they are risk-averse and driven to sustain large annual increases in profit to keep shareholders happy, they are unwilling to invest in anything with a significant risk of failure, or anything that will take more than a year or so to start generating revenues and profits.

So their idea of "innovation" is often a redesigned, repackaged, function-added, or "sequel" product, the exaggerated "new and improved" model that often turns out to be neither.

This inability to innovate is largely a cultural phenomenon. What you will find in many large corporations are these behaviors, all of which impede innovation:

- Employees hoarding rather than sharing knowledge, including knowledge that could yield innovation, to protect their positions and ranks in the company.
- Employees rarely volunteering new ideas, fearing ridicule, retribution, being ignored, or having credit for the idea stolen by their bosses if it succeeds.
- Managers safely and instinctively squelching innovative "crazy ideas" of subordinates.
- Managers, fearing the wrath of shareholders (absentee owners), are risk averse, preferring to buy ideas once they have been successfully developed by others, rather than incubating the company's own ideas, even though the latter is cheaper and more effective.
- Employees competing for credit rather than sharing it.
- Employees, since they are rated on their individual performance, considering teamwork and collaborative activities less important than individual, solitary ones.
- Managers instinctively delegating tasks in a project to individuals rather than teams (since it's easier that way to place blame if something goes wrong), and individuals usually preferring individual rather than team assignments as well.

By contrast, Natural Enterprises exhibit the following innovation-friendly behaviors:

- Decisions are made by democratic consensus rather than by fiat.
- Persuasion and change occurs by engaging decision-makers in thought processes and finding shared mental models, rather than the wielding of power and authority.
- Problem-solving teams self-form and self-manage, and select (and when necessary, change) their own leader(s) rather than having leaders imposed on them.

- Rather than formal permanent roles, positions, and "up-or-out" career paths, individuals move laterally from project to project, wherever their skills and experiences are best suited, and often wear multiple hats on simultaneously running projects, rather than having a single role.
- Recognition and appreciation are based on the depth of developed skills, experiences, learning, and networks, the things that have value to the enterprise in the future, rather than on past performance or on one's seniority or title.
- "Management" from the top down is replaced by "improvisation" throughout the organization.

Clay Christensen has come to be known for his insights on innovation, following on the heels of the late Peter Drucker, who was the first business expert to recognize the absolute inseparability of entrepreneurship and innovation.

Christensen's book *The Innovator's Solution*,[5] written with Michael Raynor, explains that entrepreneurs can create bold new opportunities for themselves through what he calls *disruptive innovations*, which dramatically alter the competitive landscape in an industry and then hold on to the competitive advantage they have achieved through what he calls *sustaining innovations*. Both are needed, and entrepreneurs must be continuously innovative to be sustainable.

Sustaining and disruptive innovations, however, are significantly different in nature, and there are two forms of the latter:

Sustaining innovations are new, high-margin, high-value products and services brought to an existing market and a known group of customers, by an incumbent company that has a strong existing relationship with those customers. Many of the new products that come from Google Labs, for example, would qualify as sustaining innovations.

Low-end disruptive innovations are those that offer a lower-cost product to a competitor's overserved customers, which the incumbent supplier doesn't care about because these overserved customers are at the low-margin end of their customer base. As technology (inevitably) improves, the disruptor gradually eats into the incumbents' primary markets from below.

Christensen and Raynor's example of this is steel minimills, which initially focused on the low-end, low-margin rebar market (which the integrated steel makers were pleased to vacate). The minimills then improved the new rebar technology and used it to move gradually upscale to the point that they have now stolen much of the high-end market (e.g., sheet steel) from the integrated giants.

To succeed at this, it's essential that the disruptive innovation *not* be initially suitable to or adaptable by the incumbents—in other words, that the incumbents don't find the disruptor's initial business model attractive. Otherwise, the incumbents will bring their considerable resources and strong customer relationships to bear to make the innovation a "sustaining" one for *them*, and ward off and defeat the disruption attempt.

Low-end disruptive innovations fill an unmet need *for a particular constituency of overserved customers.*

New market disruptive innovations are those that offer a product with benefits *previously not available at all* or *not available to most segments of customers*, and that hence create entirely new markets for new groups of customers. The personal computer and personal copier are examples of this. They both disrupted the then-existing market for large, expensive machines, and by making the benefits of computing and copying available to a much larger segment of customers, really created new industries.

New market disruptive innovations fill an unmet need *for an entirely new category of customers.*

The need/affinity matrix introduced in the previous chapter can help you think about and identify both types of disruptive innovations. Some of the columns in the matrix will be affinity groups (categories of customers) who are currently overserved by existing products. Their need (one of the rows in the matrix) is for a simpler, less expensive product than what currently exists. Some of the columns in the matrix will be affinity groups (categories of customers) who are currently not served at all by existing products. Their need (one of the rows in the matrix) is for a product or service that currently doesn't exist at all for their customer segment.

To identify customers for disruptive innovations, Christensen and Raynor say you need to look for:

- People and companies who have a need but lack the money or skill to meet it with existing products;
- People and companies who have no alternate way today to do the job your product or service could help them do; and,
- People and companies that are overserved, interested in a lower-cost, simpler product without all the extraneous and rarely used bells and whistles of current products.

It is important to keep an open mind about who your customer is. Suppose, for example, that after studying the thermal qualities of fur, feathers, and the natural anti-freeze that reptiles and amphibians produce, you have used biomimicry to innovate a new kind of inexpensive blanket that could keep the poor, homeless, and displaced warm at night in cool climates. That might well be your Natural Enterprise's Purpose.

Keep an open mind about who your customers are.

But if you were thinking of this invention as a potential disruptive innovation, you might discover that there are other markets for the technology that enabled it. Who, other than established buyers of blankets, might be interested in textiles with thermal properties? Hospitals and doctors dealing with hypothermia? Insulation companies? Gardeners and farmers seeking to protect crops from frost? Swimming-pool-cover manufacturers? Expedition outfitters? And since good thermal properties insulate against heat as well as cold, should you also consider as potential customers cooler manufacturers, refrigerator companies, umbrella makers, UV-ray protectors? The possibilities are endless.

Just like the large organizations that are constrained in their thinking by established products and customer groups, innovators can be constrained by focusing exclusively on their Purpose. Even if your Purpose is to help the poor and homeless stay warm, and you and your partners have no Passion for helping the swimming-pool industry, there may be opportunities to cross-license your thermal technology and use the royalties to pursue even more projects that *are* on Purpose for your enterprise.

Reading *The Innovator's Solution* can help give you and your partners the courage to tackle established giants, knowing that, if you use disruptive innovations, they will be helpless to respond to what you're doing. It also can give you many more real-life examples of successful and unsuccessful disruptive innovations to inspire you in your own innovation efforts.

It is important to remember that successful entrepreneurship requires *continuous* innovation. Like the winegrower and vintner quoted in the introduction of this book, you must always be striving to be "better not bigger." The innovation process described in this chapter should be a continuous process, one that is just part of the way you do business, the way you

> The innovation process should be a continuous process, one that is part of the way you do business, the way you make a living together.

make a living together. Your environmental scanning, your cultural anthropology and other research activities must continue to inform your imaginings, which in turn must continue to drive the consideration and realization of new innovations.

The resource guide at the end of the book provides articles and books that teach you more about the innovation process and different types of innovation.

We're now two-thirds of the way through the journey to Natural Entrepreneurship. You've learned how to discover what you were meant to do—what work with which partners. And you've learned how to find (through research) and fill (through innovation) unmet needs, to realize your Natural Enterprise's collective Purpose successfully, employ your Gifts, and engage your Passions.

In the final two chapters of this book, you'll learn how to make this success sustainable. The keys to doing this are *improvisation, resilience, responsiveness, responsibility*, and *relationships*.

CHAPTER 4 CASE STUDY
Innovation is everyone's job, every day

WL Gore

WL Gore, the company that invented Gore-Tex waterproof, breathable, weather-resistant fabrics, has a long history of deep and continuous innovation. *Fast Company* magazine has rated them the United States's most innovative company.

Some of those innovations are characteristic of a Natural Enterprise, and, since the company is relatively large ($2 billion annual revenues), they have provided a wonderful proving ground for the scalability of Natural Enterprise concepts and principles.

The company calls itself a "nonhierarchical corporation."

The secrets of the company's success, all of them entirely consistent with the principles of Natural Enterprise, are:

- The Power of Small Teams: WL Gore tries to keep its teams small (and caps even its manufacturing plants at two hundred people). That way, everyone can get to know one another and work together with minimal rules, as though they were a task force tackling a crisis.
- No Ranks, No Titles, No Bosses: Associates (employees) select mentors, they don't have bosses. Associates decide for themselves what new commitments to take on. Committees evaluate

an associate's contribution and decide on compensation. There are no standardized job descriptions or categories.

- Take the LongView: WL Gore is impatient with the status quo but patient about the time—often years, sometimes decades—it takes to develop revolutionary products and bring them to market.
- Make Time for Face Time: There's no hierarchical chain of command; anyone in the company can talk to anyone else. WL Gore discourages memos and prefers in-person communication to e-mail.
- Innovation Is Everyone's Job: Associates spend 10 percent of their time pursuing speculative new ideas. Anyone is free to launch a project, so long as they have the passion and ideas to attract collaborators. Many of WL Gore's breakthroughs started with one person acting on his or her own initiative, and developed as colleagues helped in their spare time.
- Celebrate Failure: Don't stigmatize it. When a project doesn't work out and the team kills it, they celebrate with beer or champagne.

Some critics are now questioning WL Gore's environmental credentials, since Gore-Tex is a derivative of Teflon, the controversial chemical used in cookware that many believe poses a health hazard. Time will tell whether WL Gore has the resilience and innovation to overcome this threat to its reputation.

. . . .

CHAPTER 4 CASE STUDY
Sustainable ideas to meet the need for zero waste

Interface Carpets

(Full disclosure: The author is a small shareholder in this company.)

The founder of Interface Carpets, Ray Anderson, has a mission:

> I believe we have come to the threshold of the next indus-
> trial revolution. At Interface, we seek to become the first
> sustainable corporation in the world, and, following that, the
> first restorative company. It means creating the technolo-
> gies of the future—kinder, gentler technologies that emulate
> nature's systems. I believe that's where we will find the
> right model. Ultimately, I believe we must learn to depend
> solely on available income the way a forest does, not on
> our precious stores of natural capital. Linear practices must
> be replaced by cyclical ones. That's nature's way. In nature,
> there is no waste; one organism's waste is another's food. For
> our industrial process, so dependent on petrochemical, man-
> made raw materials, this means technical "food" reincarnated
> by recycling into the product's next life cycle. Of course, the
> recycling operations will have to be driven by solar energy,
> too. We look forward to the day when our factories have no
> smokestacks and no effluents. If successful, we'll spend the
> rest of our days harvesting yesteryear's carpets, recycling old
> petrochemicals into new materials, and converting sunlight
> into energy. There will be zero scrap going into landfills and
> zero emissions into the biosphere. Literally, our company
> will grow by cleaning up the world, not by polluting or
> degrading it. We'll be doing well by doing good. That's the
> vision. Is it a dream? Certainly, but it is a dream we share
> with our 5,000 associates, our vendors, and our customers.
> Everyone will have to dream this dream to make it a reality,
> but until then, we are committed to leading the way.

The company, one of the largest commercial and industrial carpet
manufacturers on the planet, is well on its way to becoming the first
large, public Natural Enterprise. It has already substantially achieved
its "cradle-to-cradle" zero-waste, zero-emissions, 100 percent-
reused-or-recycled target.

Here are some other things it does:

- Sustainability priorities: Eliminating waste, benign emissions, renewable energy, technology innovation, resource-efficient transportation, sensitizing shareholders, and redesigning commerce for sustainability.
- Takes back and reuses or recycles almost everything it sells.
- Employs biomimicry processes—learning from nature how to make things naturally, in its innovation programs.
- Publishes a sustainability report to all citizens of the world, and especially its customers, "associates" (not "employees"), and residents of the communities in which it operates; the company considers the sustainability report more important than its report to shareholders.
- Provides dedicated time for associates to spend in activities, often sponsored by the company, with their families.
- Invests heavily in social and environmental programs in the communities in which it operates.
- Measures itself on seven scales of success, only one of which is financial performance.
- Has adopted the principles of Natural Capitalism, a broad set of principles toward sustainable production leading to zero net impact on the planet.
- Has developed a model for enterprises in the twenty-first century—Natural Enterprises—that contrasts sharply with the typical model of corporations in the twentieth century and dedicated itself to becoming the prototype of this new model.

PART THREE

MAKING IT SUSTAINABLE

THE RESILIENCE OF NATURAL ENTERPRISE

We'd prefer not to have our name put into nomination for any entrepreneurial awards. To be honest, we don't really work that hard, we're not that smart, and we make a really good living while having a hell of a lot of fun. I think most other entrepreneurs would be irritated if we won. Let them win the award. They probably deserve it for all they've had to go through.

—Anonymous co-CEO of a $250 million enterprise.

The previous four chapters have explained how to discover what you were meant to do (and with whom), and how to do it (through excellent research and innovation processes).

Successful Natural Enterprises have two additional essential ingredients. First, they have the ability to improvise, to keep the organization agile, sustainable, and resilient (the subject of this chapter), and they have the values and processes that create and sustain strong, open, collaborative relationships and nurture responsiveness and responsibility in the people in those relationships—your enterprise partners, your business allies, your customers, and the community in which you live and operate (the subject of the next, final chapter).

> Successful Natural Enterprises have two additional essential ingredients: the ability to improvise, and the values and processes that create and sustain strong, open, collaborative relationships.

Before explaining what improvisation is, and why it's so important, though, it's probably worthwhile recapping the differences between traditional corporations (set up and operated according to conventional wisdom) and Natural Enterprises (set up and operated according to the principles, practices, and processes outlined in this book).

What makes Natural Enterprises different?

I've been talking about Natural Enterprise throughout this book, and you probably have a pretty good sense by now of what it's about. Now it's time to define it.

Natural Enterprise: A sustainable, self-organized, self-managed, community-based business partnership in which a group of people agree to make a living together as collaborators and peers, strive to attain what each member needs to achieve for his or her personal well-being, accept substantial responsibility for each other, and respect and help the community or communities in which the enterprise operates and the natural environment. It is "natural" because this form of socioeconomic activity occurs ubiquitously in hunter-gatherer cultures and in most nonhuman animal cultures.

Here's how Natural Enterprises are different from traditional corporations:

The first two of these differences were addressed in Part 1 and Part 2 of this book respectively. In this chapter, I'll explain differences 3 through 7, while differences 8 and 9 will be explained in the next chapter.

This list of nine critical differences between traditional corporations and Natural Enterprises emerged from my study of the more than 150 clients I have served over three decades, in the attempt to explain why some of those clients seemed to operate so successfully, so *effortlessly*.

This list was vindicated at a recent symposium on the Organization of the Future, which asked some forward-thinking executives to describe the type of organization they thought was ideally suited to meet the business challenges of the twenty-first century. Here are

	Traditional Corporation	Natural Enterprise
1. People: recruitment and motivational process	Hire talent through competitive salaries, set ever-higher performance expectations and reward strictly on recent performance	Find partners with shared Purposes and complementary Gifts and Passions, co-evolve meaningful work, and give people what they need
2. Product/service development process	Develop new products in a "lab," mass produce, turn over to sales & marketing	Listen to customers, identify unmet needs, imagine (and study nature), and innovate solutions to these needs through continuous parallel experiments with your customers
3. Modus operandi (operating method)	Analyze, prescribe reality-changing solutions	Enable understanding to emerge, identify adaptive approaches
4. Organizational structure	Hierarchical, with instructions flowing down and information flowing up	Flat, networked, self-directed, egalitarian, collaborative, with ideas and information shared peer to peer
5. Sources of capital and funding	Infusions of external capital, with control substantially ceded to shareholder-investors at the "cost of capital"	Organic, from customers and reinvested earnings, with full control retained by the partners
6. Marketing process	Advertise and market to "create" demand and "need"	Viral (word-of-mouth) marketing, through delighted customers
7. How success is measured	Short-term rate of growth and return on investment (ROI) to shareholders	Long-term, sustainable well-being of partners, customers, and community
8. Relationship to others in the community	Develop product in lab, mass produce, advertise to "create" needs	Identify unmet customer need, develop customized solution, deliver to prequalified customers, market virally
9. Basis of relationship to customers and competitors	Political and economic power; competitiveness; brand presence; size, market domination	Collaboration, customer intimacy, strength of reciprocal networks, strong communication

the attributes[1] they came up with, which are indeed the attributes of a Natural Enterprise. It is an organization that:

- is less like an army (hierarchical, focused on winning) and more like a family/community (collaborative, focused on well-being of members) than today's large organizations
- is better able to deal with complexity
- has a flexible definition of "work" that is purposeful and meaningful to its people
- is accessible, inclusive, and diverse
- is responsive to the communities in which it operates
- is self-managed, innovative, and entrepreneurial
- generates deep mutual respect and trust in its people
- is resilient and agile, and capable of "acting in the moment"
- attracts people skilled at collaboration and inclined to work collaboratively
- has a self-determined, shared set of values
- is committed to "not being evil"
- is amoeba-like (permeable borders, good sensors, able to change shape when necessary, a strong guiding nucleus, and replicable)
- is attuned to and responsive to customer needs (rather than trying to sell them something they don't really need or want)
- accommodates needs and conflicting demands of its people, using principles of reciprocity
- motivates and engages its people
- cross-pollinates people, ideas, knowledge, and points of view
- is transparent and authentic
- is not location-based or location-dependent
- uses sustainable, cradle-to-cradle practices, and does more with less
- engages customers and other partners in design, development, and decision-making, to tap into the wisdom of crowds
- accommodates and leverages the skills and qualities of women
- finds and clears away obstacles that prevent its people from doing their best

- learns from nature
- teaches people to communicate extraordinarily well, and encourages authentic, powerful conversations
- recognizes our responsibility to leave a legacy for our children and pays attention to them and learns from them

Sounds like a great place to work, doesn't it? Let's take a look at some of these attributes, attributes that "naturally" tend to arise in enterprises that are created and operated using the principles, practices, and processes outlined earlier in this book.

The following six Natural Enterprise attributes all contribute to making the organization more *resilient*—able to withstand unforeseen, *unforeseeable* changes.

Six attributes of a resilient organization: Improvisation, self-management, organic financing, viral marketing, measuring success differently, and staying small

Improvisation and enterprise agility

When the terrorist attacks of 9/11 happened, an entrepreneur in my community near Toronto, who makes modular portable buildings, knew what he had to do.

He phoned a couple of small trucking colleagues—not the big multinational truckers, but guys who, like himself, could turn their businesses on a dime. Within a few hours, several truckloads of portable building components, with an assembly crew riding shotgun, were on their way to Ground Zero.

Much of the paperwork was written by hand as they were driving. The truckers contacted their customs brokers at the border to tell them what they were doing. Not only were they not stopped at the border like everyone else, they had a personal two-country police escort to hustle them past the traffic jams and across into New York State.

When they got to Ground Zero, somehow the rescue workers

knew they were coming, cleared them space, gave them masks, and let them get to work. The buildings were constructed before any of the larger, local competitors had a chance to even react, and they were used extensively for makeshift housing, medical stations, and supply depots for weeks.

The company received a special citation from the City of New York. They got a ton of free publicity and their business continues to boom several years later.

Part altruism, part instinct, all *improvisation*. When interviewed, the president of the small company said "We didn't even think about it. We just acted. We just kind of made it up as we went along."

> **Improvisation is key to resilience, because it allows agility in reacting quickly and effectively to unforeseen, unforeseeable events.**

The word *improvisation* comes from the Latin word meaning "unforeseen." Improvisation is key to resilience, because it allows agility in reacting quickly and effectively to unforeseen, unforeseeable events.

How do you make your organization improvisational and agile?

First, respect and trust your partners, your customers, and those in your community and your networks

Then, make sure you have the twelve essential capacities of entrepreneurship (summarized in the introduction of this book on pages 18–21), especially imagination and creativity, in your organization, and that each of your partners knows who has each capacity, so that the right people can be recognized and called upon when unforeseen situations arise.

If nothing else, experiment: Keep trying out different things, tools, processes, techniques, and practices. Never lose your ability to learn fast and "fail fast" (give up on experiments that are not working before they become expensive investments, and learn from the failures).

Finally, practice makes perfect. Whether you're improvising in a jazz combo or preparing for the next pandemic, it's rehearsal, exercise, and practice that make you ready for the unforeseen, not planning.

You should pay attention—listen, observe, and notice what's going on around you, and understand why it's happening. If you've set up a continuous environmental scan for your research (Chapter 3), it also can help you anticipate possibilities before they're on others' radar. Along with that, you should have alternatives prepared. Your Natural Enterprise needs to have alternatives available if, say, interest rates spike, the value of the dollar plummets, oil goes to $160 a barrel, or climate change makes food and paper ten times more expensive. This means you need to be organized for agility—don't be dependent on any one person or any one function, and be able to redeploy people and resources easily and quickly, such as when a crisis occurs and new needs suddenly emerge.

To succeed you will need to develop organizational instinct and emotional intelligence—the ability to sense what's coming next, what someone really feels that they may not yet be articulating, and know how best to respond.

One way to learn is to learn from nature—no one can teach you and show you how to improvise better than someone who's been doing it for billions of years.

Most of all, use scenarios. Think ahead to what might happen—a severe economic recession, a currency collapse, or an enduring water shortage, for example—and decide which scenarios are most likely and what you would do if each actually happened. Don't lock yourself in to one scenario by overcommitting or getting overextended or overleveraged.[2]

Self-management

The term "self-management" applies at both the personal and collective enterprise level, and at both levels practicing it can increase resilience. At the personal level, self-management entails:[3]

- Setting your own personal goals, performance objectives, and challenging but realistic expectations
- Figuring out what you need to do to achieve these goals: Concrete, measurable, (self-)manageable steps

- Making a personal *commitment* to do them, keeping that commitment, and giving yourself credit for keeping it
- Evaluating your own performance (the product of your talent, skills, commitment, energy, and alignment with your Gifts and Passions) and its results
- Rewarding yourself for high personal performance (regardless of what the outcome was, since that outcome is likely to be due to factors beyond your control)

Your organization, and project teams within it, can also practice self-management. This entails taking ownership of and responsibility for problems as they arise, self-organizing to involve the right people to address them, creatively and critically thinking them through and achieving consensus, and then acting accordingly. When you and your partners do this, you're going to be more resilient in the face of unforeseen occurrences than if you wait for the person "whose job it is" to address these occurrences.

Organic financing

Organic financing is generating the funds you need to start and operate your enterprise without resorting to external sources of capital (share offerings, venture capitalists, banks, etc.). This entails working with customers and partners, not shareholders and investors, to find the short-term cash you need to fund operations from the point of purchase of raw materials and supplies to the point of receipt of cash from satisfied customers, what is called "working capital," and using similar creative techniques to prevent the need to borrow or otherwise acquire "strings-attached" funds from outside organizations for equipment, premises, and other long-term capital needs.

Let's take a look at the three types of financing that traditional businesses use, and see how Natural Enterprises handle them.

1. Seed Capital: This is the most difficult and expensive type of capital to raise. It is used for purposes like the set-up of premises and tooling of equipment, development of prototypes, initial

advertising, promotion, legal and professional services, licenses, and similar start-up costs. Most of this money is spent before the company begins receiving any cash from product sales. These costs are almost always underestimated, and actually represent start-up losses that many new businesses never recover from. Financing organically is the process of minimizing or even eliminating these losses. This can be done by:

- Doing your own research and legwork thoroughly in advance (rather than paying others to do it), meeting with potential customers, prequalifying and taking advance orders (and if possible, deposits) for product before you start up, so that you know what, and how much, will sell and at what price—no wasted out-of-pocket expenditures need be incurred, no unsalable product need be made, and some customers may be persuaded to advance funds for first shipments of products in return for a one-time price discount.

- Growing more slowly: Reinvesting the profits from one month's sales to finance the operations of the next month, so that the business literally "pays for itself."

- Allowing the enterprise's partners to choose their own mix of up-front investment: Depending on how each partner values his or her time, some partners will prefer to invest lots of time doing the up-front research, while others who value their time more highly may prefer to provide some seed capital to the enterprise in return for a lower personal time investment.

- Drawing on the community: There are a lot of people in every community who have money invested in low-return securities. They might be persuaded to invest some of it in a local community-based business that they know has been well researched (and that they can personally help to make successful) and that will also give them a higher return than fixed-income securities. In some jurisdictions, credit unions may offer preferential terms to local enterprises. Some communities even have financial co-ops, nonprofit member-owned Natural Financial Enterprises that provide short-term loans and financial advisory services to local enterprises.

- Viral marketing: Letting your customers market your product for you, instead of paying for expensive advertising. More on this in a moment.
- Budgeting carefully: In many cases, you can save up-front cash by doing things yourself, using professionals you know (sparingly) as advisors instead of paid suppliers, deferring discretionary expenditures, making do with smaller, fewer, or without, and still run a professional-looking business. Women may be better at this than are men; this is borne out by their superior survival rates as entrepreneurs.

2. Capital Financing: Leasing instead of buying allows you to amortize the costs and the cash outflows over the same period as the revenues, so you need no "long-term" capital loans. Or, as with seed capital, an older, cash-rich partner may choose to contribute capital assets to the enterprise in exchange for investing fewer hours into it, so the cost of capital to the enterprise is very low but the ROI to the investing partner is better than he or she can get in the bank.

3. Working Capital Financing: Receivables can be sold or "factored" to a bank on a revolving short-term basis, essentially converting these assets into cash that can be used to pay current liabilities to suppliers. Inventories in most entrepreneurial businesses are negligible, since most such businesses make products to custom specifications and on a just-in-time basis—the inventory is only bought or made when it has already been sold, so the customer effectively finances it.

There are many other creative ways of funding the business when it cannot be financed organically. With a cautious spending strategy and reinvestment of profits, most Natural Enterprises shouldn't need to borrow often, or for long periods, or have to give up equity at all.

Viral marketing

Viral marketing entails using your customers as your sales force to spread the word about your products and services.

With every additional business scandal, the public becomes more cynical about advertising, PR, and product claims. The concept of viral marketing is not new: A decade ago, Jeff Rayport of *Fast Company* introduced its six fundamental principles:[4]

- Use stealth and subtlety to convey your message,
- Give stuff away free up-front,
- Exploit peer-to-peer networks to spread the message,
- Make the message memorable and "sticky,"
- Exploit the strength of weak ties, and
- Work to reach a "tipping point."

A few years ago, Rayport's message caught fire when Malcolm Gladwell's book *The Tipping Point*[5] became a best seller, provided more detailed evidence of how well and how broadly these six principles work, and gave detailed instructions on how to employ them. These two factors—the increased distrust of corporate messages and the new recipe for "doing" viral marketing, are taking viral marketing mainstream—it's no longer just a technique for those who can't afford advertising, but a technique to replace advertising.

Using these principles isn't difficult, risky, expensive, or demanding of great patience or energy.

One of the biggest land mines for entrepreneurs is getting into "copycat" businesses where it is next to impossible to differentiate your product or service from the next person's. And the innovation process starts with listening to the (current or prospective) customer. So if you've done your research, and you have a small group of customers who agree that your product or service is innovative—better or cheaper or faster or in some way significantly distinguishable from everyone else's—then all you need to do is to deliver to that group of customers, and let *them* be your marketing team.

As Gladwell's *The Tipping Point* describes, some of the most success-ful books and recordings, some of the most infectious ideas, and some of the fastest-growing new products, such as TiVo, basically found their market with almost no money spent on advertising or promotion.

You can get the impression from browsing the Internet that viral marketing is a Web-based advertising process, or even that it involves mass e-mailing. Not true. It is nothing more than spreading the word about your product or service by customer word of mouth. Talk to the most successful contractors you know, and you'll likely find they turn away excess business and do no advertising or stuffing of mailboxes. Their new customers come entirely from referrals from existing satisfied customers. They do no selling and no marketing.

This brings us to the most critical precondition for successful viral marketing: *Reputation.* Nothing will sabotage and choke off viral-marketing success faster than a sudden reputation for poor quality or poor service.

Probably the most important of Rayport's six principles is the fourth one: making your message memorable and "sticky." Viral marketing requires your product or service to come up in your customers' conversations with others. That means, as with TiVo, there needs to be something about it that people will want to talk about.

Measuring success differently

Traditional corporations measure success in terms of short-term growth in revenues and return on investment. This is because these corporations are beholden to their shareholders, who may well not be involved with, knowledgeable about, or concerned with the busi-ness at all.

Because Natural Enterprises are not private-benefit shareholder-owned corporations, but instead partnerships or cooperatives[6] that are owned equally by the partners/members, they can choose their own measures of success, on their own terms.

The measures they choose will depend on what they care about individually and collectively, and what they need (to be able to afford to continue doing the work of the Natural Enterprise, work that allows them to apply their Gifts and Passions to work that is "on Purpose" for them). These measures *may* include:

1. Generation of enough cash from the enterprise to meet the personal cash needs of the partners and sustain the enterprise through reinvestment to replace its productive capacity,
2. Ability of the partners to limit and "flex" their working hours so as to pursue other interests, responsibilities, and passions that are important to them,
3. Partners' assessment of their happiness doing what they're doing.
4. Customers' delight with the offerings of the enterprise,
5. The extent to which the operations of the enterprise are realizing the enterprise's Purpose,
6. Adherence to the enterprise's Principles (discussed in the introduction and the next chapter),
7. Extent to which the enterprise contributes to the well-being of the community in which it operates.

By using such measures, and allowing these measures to direct the decision making of the enterprise, Natural Enterprises are able to weather economic ups and downs and stay focused on the needs of customers and community. This focus is the real reason the enterprise exists, its Purpose. As a result, its decisions are going to be "on Purpose" and focused on the longer term, rather than dictated by the short-term expectations of external shareholders who have little or no interest in the long-term sustainability of the enterprise. Inevitably, then, Natural Enterprises will be more resilient, more durable, more capable of investing in their longer-term interest, and hence more sustainable.

Staying small

Most large corporations need to grow profits each year to keep their shareholders happy. That means, generally, they need to grow revenues too, which means they have to keep expanding, introducing major new products, or acquiring smaller companies. They become extremely vulnerable, then, to market shocks.

By contrast, Natural Enterprises don't need to grow bigger to survive. Like the winery mentioned in the introduction, they can focus on getting better instead. The fact that they can do very well just staying the same size gives them, relative to traditional corporations, a lot of resilience against market downturns, commodity-price or interest-rate spikes, and material shortages.

> **Natural Enterprises don't need to grow bigger to survive. They can focus on getting better instead.**

By focusing on customers, and getting better instead of bigger, they are better attuned to shifts in customer demand, needs, and buying criteria.

Let's return to our Really Simple Technologies case study. The first five of the above six attributes of resilient organizations would seem to be "natural" for RST. But the sixth, staying small, could be a real challenge.

How could RST stay small and resilient if they need to produce tens of millions of units of their switchable solar/electric home lighting systems, for example? They could offshore production to a struggling nation, and reduce labor and overhead costs, but then they'd be vulnerable to spikes in shipping costs and the political stability of the nation where their products were made.

A better answer might be to license the technology to hundreds of small, local, entrepreneurial manufacturers who could produce their products close to the customer base. If one of the manufacturers closed, they could just switch to the next closest one. They might even help all these local manufacturers organize into a cooperative like the Mondragon[7] cooperative in Spain that brokers the work of thousands of cottage industries and local entrepreneurs. And in this way, they might discover that they were then being supplied by a network of other Natural Enterprises, small local companies whose Gifts, Passions, and Purposes intersected precisely where needed to be capable and enthusiastic manufacturers of the products RST invents.

In this way, RST could stay small and reinvest the license fees to invent even more technologies "on Purpose" for them.

The myths of entrepreneurship

There are hundreds of books on the market on how to start a traditional small business. Most of them reinforce myths that date back to the earliest days of the Industrial Economy and corporate charters. Many of them focus on the "mechanics" of small business—what form of organization to choose, what records to keep and statements to prepare and filings to make, but nothing about the art and practice of entrepreneurship.

Likewise, university courses on entrepreneurship are often case-study-driven, academic programs that focus on specific business strategies, management approaches, and "leadership" styles.

As a result of all of these books and courses, it's not surprising that a number of myths about entrepreneurship have arisen and prevailed despite evidence that they're just wrong. Many of them are reflected in the Ten Fears of Entrepreneurship that I mentioned in the introduction: That it takes an extraordinary combination of skills and talents all wrapped up in one person, that it's stressful, lonely, exhausting, expensive, risky, complicated, and requires incredible self-confidence, creativity, perseverance, lots of external capital, constant growth, intensive and expensive marketing, a franchising "formula," financial acumen, nerves of steel, and extraordinary management skill and experience.

By now you should appreciate that these fears, and the related myths about entrepreneurship, stem from the fact most entrepreneurs practice *un*-Natural Entrepreneurship—and make it much harder and less enjoyable than it has to be.

There are three other long-standing myths that are worth looking at—and exploding—as well.

Myth #1

There's a talent shortage, and you have to pay big money—more than any entrepreneur can afford—to attract good people. What there really is is a *Passion* shortage. Many in the workforce rush home from their boring jobs to invest hours each evening doing what they love doing—and pay for the privilege. I've never met an outstandingly talented individual who wouldn't be willing to work for just enough to live on, if he or she had a real Passion for the work.

Myth #2

Every organization needs hierarchy, someone in charge. The reason we're so skeptical of self-organized and self-managed systems is that we have no practice or experience with them. Read the stories in this book about Semco or WL Gore and discover that even fairly large organizations can thrive without hierarchy.

Myth #3

If you want to be in business, you have to give up your soul. I know many altruistic, caring people who are working in huge institutions (health care, education, public service, charitable organizations, etc.) because they're convinced that the alternative, "private" enterprise, is inherently evil, greedy, acquisitive, morally reprehensible, and even pathological. Because these huge institutions are often bureaucratic and ineffective, these altruists have given up hope of ever finding meaningful work. The stories in this book about Briarpatch, South Mountain, Good Energy, Tall Grass Prairie Bread, Mountain Equipment, and Interface Carpets should be enough to convince you that Natural Enterprise need not cost you your soul, and just might help you find it again.

CHAPTER 5 CASE STUDY
Organically financed, virally marketed, and on Purpose

Good Energy

Neil Crofts' *Authentic Business*[8] profiles several businesses that qualify as Natural Enterprises. One of them is Good Energy, a business established by the British entrepreneur Juliet Davenport.

Juliet's Gifts include exceptional knowledge of atmospheric physics and environmental economics. Her Purpose is to make the world more habitable, without requiring people to sacrifice their lifestyles.

What distinguishes Good Energy from other energy supply companies?

- They meet an expressed need from environmentally conscious British consumers and businesses for 100 percent renewable energy.
- They were financed organically by six hundred customers.
- Their ten thousand customers are their salespeople and "evangelists."
- They are community-based, so they live with and intimately know their customers, and feel a powerful sense of responsibility to them.
- They have developed an innovative peer-production scheme—they buy energy from homes in their community that produce their own solar or wind energy.
- They have developed strong reciprocal networks with champions of renewable energy.
- They are driven to innovate their technologies continuously so that, as prices for nonrenewable energy rises, the price for their energy will fall.

Major decisions are made at "Gaia meetings" that assess those decisions against the sustainability and "more habitable world" operating principles of the enterprise.

· ·

CHAPTER 5 CASE STUDY
Self-management in action

Semco SA

When Ricardo Semler took over his father's Brazilian business, he decided to transform it into a nonhierarchical, self-managed organization run by its employees. The industrial machinery company has been wildly successful ever since, but to Semler, the point isn't profit, it's meaningful work, the chance to learn, and to allow everyone to be entrepreneurial.

Semler has said he doesn't care whether the company is five times or one fifth the current size in the future. It's up to the workers to decide where they want to take the company, and whatever they decide, and whatever that leads to, is fine with him. The three thousand workers each have one vote.

Work hours, salaries, and working conditions are all decided by the workers, collaboratively. Semler does not intervene. The workers switch jobs to broaden their skills and understanding of the overall business of the company.

Semco's plants feature hammocks for afternoon naps. There are no policy manuals, dress codes, mission statements, or organization charts. The company is entirely improvisational. Semler believes this is the only way to create organizational resilience in the face of the turmoil of Brazil's economy and the imposing challenges of the global economy in the years ahead.

The company has no offices and no administrative assistants. It's virtually devoid of bureaucracy. Semler believes that management authority in any organization is illusory—that people will do what they will do, in the best interests of the company, and find work-arounds when necessary to do so. So the best things for managers to do, he believes, is to stay out of the way.

. . . .

RESPONSIBILITY, COLLABORATION, RELATIONSHIP, COMMUNITY
the power of people

In the long history of humankind, those who learned to collaborate and improvise most effectively have always prevailed.

—Charles Darwin

We've arrived at the final chapter in the journey to Natural Entrepreneurship. In previous chapters, we've covered how to find the "sweet spot" where your Gifts, Passions, and Purpose intersect—the work you're meant to do, and the people you're meant to do it with. We've covered the research and innovation processes, and ways to make your Natural Enterprise resilient.

In this last chapter, we'll look at the importance and power of people in Natural Enterprise, and how, by nurturing strong, trusted relationships, you can create an enterprise that is not only natural but also indomitable.

The power of responsibility, responsiveness, and reputation

As explained in Chapter 2, one of the critical steps in finding the people you want to make a living with in Natural Enterprise is agreement on a Statement of Operating Principles. For Really Simple Technologies, the case study we have been using throughout this book, these Operating Principles were:

- No managers, hierarchy, or titles,
- Only long-term qualitative measures,
- Commitment to service,
- No secrecy,
- Compensation based on need, not performance,
- Decision making by unanimous consensus and by empowerment of individual partners,
- Sustainability and size limit,
- Buy local,
- High social and environmental responsibility,
- Work isn't everything,
- No absentee ownership,
- Responsibility to partners, customers, and community.

These principles address behaviors, rewards, values, decision-making guidelines, and interactions with people.

They include responsibility to three groups: partners, customers, and the community in which the enterprise operates, and refer specifically to social and environmental sustainability. One of the hottest topics today in the investment community (especially among long-term investment managers such as pension funds), in meetings of boards of directors (since boards are responsible for the effective stewardship of corporations), and in conferences on the future of business is the issue of the social and environmental responsibility of organizations.

The day in which corporations were considered responsible only to their shareholders is fast disappearing as the role of corporations in socially and environmentally devastating activities such as global warming, offshoring jobs to third-world nations, and releasing emissions responsible for chronic diseases is coming to public attention. The *reputation* of corporations is now the Number Two risk issue keeping their CEOs awake at night (business continuity is Number One), according to recent surveys.

Compare the reputation of ExxonMobil to that of Interface Carpets and it doesn't take long to see that reputation is tied directly to whom you show a sense of responsibility to, whom your behavior shows you care about and respond to. ExxonMobil has shrugged off (and refused to acknowledge or pay for) its responsibility for the horrific *Exxon Valdez* oil spill, and more recently for its role as the world's leading producer of greenhouse gases producing climate change. Why? Because ExxonMobil considers itself responsible only to its shareholders. It believes it is fully justified in "externalizing" the social and environmental costs of its activities (leaving them for negatively affected citizens, taxpayers, insurance companies, employees, and devastated communities to "pay for") because not taking responsibility and not responding to demands for better corporate behavior *is what its shareholders want.*

Your organization's sense of responsibility to those affected by it—in the case of Natural Enterprises, notably its partners (or, if it's a cooperative, its members), its customers, and the community in which it operates—dictates substantially what it does, what decisions it makes, and how it behaves, and reflects its chosen Purpose.

What's more, your sense of responsibility and responsiveness, and your reputation, determine the value of your enterprise's *social capital.* In business parlance, social capital is a form of intangible or intellectual capital. As we move from an industrial economy to a knowledge economy, social capital—the "value" of your relationships with your partners, customers, and community—is increasing rapidly. Social capital confers several benefits that don't accrue to shareholder-benefit corporations who are only "responsible" to their shareholders:

> Social capital–the "value" of your relationships with your partners, customers, and community–confers benefits that don't accrue to corporations who are only "responsible" to their shareholders.

- Willingness of customers to pay a premium for its products, and buy more of its products, because these customers "feel good" about buying from socially and environmentally responsible organizations,

- Open, positive communications with customers and communities, leading to a better appreciation of their needs and a relationship that enables codevelopment of new products and coresolution of any problems,
- The rewards of viral marketing, as customers and communities spread the good word about what the organization is doing, and about its products and services (worth more than advertising and promotion, and less expensive),
- Access to low-cost, no-strings-attached funds from altruistic financial organizations, foundations, "angel" investors, and customers who prefer to invest their money with organizations that care about more than short-term profits, and
- A better reputation, and hence less risk that governments and the public will pursue legislation, legal action, boycotts, or other actions to curtail what is seen as misbehavior.

Studies of the "market value" of public corporations suggests that social capital may now be the largest single component of the market value of shares. This suggests that the value of social capital, and of being responsible and responsive to your people, your customers, and your community, is real, not just "the right thing to do." Reputation may not yet be "everything" in business, but it clearly pays huge dividends.

The power of collaboration and cooperation

Collaboration is *working together to achieve collective results that the individuals would be incapable of accomplishing working alone.*

When you work together toward a shared goal with your enterprise partners and with your customers and members of your community, you can get synergies of effort that working separately, or competitively,

> Collaboration is working together to achieve collective results that the individuals would be incapable of accomplishing working alone.

or adversarially, cannot achieve. At the peak of their productivity, the Beatles collaboratively produced music that none of them could ever had produced working alone or serially.

You can see the genius of collaboration in some of the world's greatest literature (T. S. Eliot's poetry was largely the result of the collaboration of three people), the extraordinary performance of some sports teams that lack superstars but whose players seem to know each other so well and work together so well that they appear to operate as a single intelligent organism. I've seen astonishing results coming out of brainstorming collaborations, neighborhood barn-raisings, jam sessions, theater, and comedy improv.

Great collaborations seem to have four essential ingredients.

1. The collaborators know, trust, and even love each other.
2. There is considerable diversity of knowledge, talent, experience, and point of view among the collaborators, which can be brought to bear on the collaborative work, enabling an enormous amount of learning to occur during the collaboration.
3. The communication that occurs during the collaboration is constant, candid, interactive, open, and constructive, involving all collaborators equally. Excellent collaborators tend to be excellent conversationalists.
4. The collaborators have had a lot of practice collaborating. So much human activity today is individual or spectator activity. Most modern work is solitary by design. Our recreational activities are either competitive or passive instead of cooperative and participatory. So it takes some practice to relearn our instinctive capacity to collaborate.

Almost everything about Natural Enterprise is inherently collaborative: finding the partners you were meant to make a living with, development of your shared Vision and Operating Principles, the interplay of cultural anthropology and the sharing of discoveries in your research, the practice of ideation and the brainstorming and other activities involved in business innovation, the process of improvisation, and the marketing of your offerings virally. Learning and practicing the art of collaboration is essential to Natural Enterprise success.

Collaboration is ideally suited to enable the emergence of understanding and the realization of what needs to be done in today's complex environments and systems. Nothing is ever as simple as it seems, in business as everywhere else. Traditional industrial corporations all too often assign the critical work of understanding, analyzing, ideation, and decision-making to individuals, and the lack of collaboration often shows in the disastrous results.

Besides engendering the four essential ingredients of collaboration listed above, there are a few more things you can do to make your enterprise and its people and activities more collaborative.

First, get your people involved in truly collaborative activities. Once you and your collaborators have experienced that remarkable feeling of collective accomplishment, they'll be hooked and will want to practice it regularly and learn to do it better. Not only are such activities fun, they're extraordinary learning experiences, too.

Then, provide infrastructure—facilitation, coaching, and learning resources—to your partners and collaborators that help them succeed and become *instinctively* better at it.

You also should help collaborators self-select and self-manage. Oust the big egos and out the wallflowers and lurkers.

Finally, be vocal when a project or activity that could or should be collaborative, is not, either because it's set up too hierarchically or because some of the "players" don't behave in egalitarian, collaborative ways.

The resource guide at the end of the book suggests additional readings to improve your organization's ability to collaborate.

The power of relationships:
partnership, networks, alliances, and reciprocity

Two fundamental principles of business are: Relationships trump credentials in buying and many other business decisions, and it's not what you know, it's *who* you know that counts.

Relationships are the essential currency of enterprise, the lubricant of exchange without which business would be constrained and limited by self-interest.

The fact that Natural Enterprises are true partnerships (or cooperatives, which are a special form of partnership) sends an important message to all the people your enterprise seeks to form and build relationships with. Partnerships are essentially *cooperative relationships of equals.* By contrast, traditional corporations are inherently *competitive hierarchical relationships of power.*

When you introduce your Natural Enterprise as a partnership, you are telling others that you understand the value of partnership, cooperation, equality among peers, and reciprocity. The fact that you run your own enterprise on that basis engenders trust in those you meet that your relationship with them will operate on the same basis. This is an important advantage over traditional corporations in forging new business relationships.

Because who you know is more important than what you know, networking, the process of building and nurturing business relationships, is an essential entrepreneurial competency.

Powerful networks let you:

- Improve knowledge about customer needs,
- Increase customer trust,
- Find new customers, volunteers, and low-cost, short-term cash,
- Increase your knowledge about markets and good business practices,
- Get answers to questions and business problems inexpensively,
- Market test new products or service ideas virally,
- Get your best customers to spread the word about your

credentials and expertise virally (much more effective than self-promotion),

- Find new suppliers, contractors, partners, advisors, or coaches,
- Conduct informal surveys to tap into the Wisdom of Crowds,
- Collaborate informally on open-source or other projects.

Although there are many social-networking tools available to help you network online, these tools are, so far, not very effective or easy to use. The best networking still entails face-to-face contact, ideally one-on-one, and the only tool needed is a good contact list or a Rolodex.

I've been teaching courses on social-networking tools for the last few years, and if you're interested in exploring them (provided it's not at the cost of face-to-face networking) here are the ones I'd most recommend:

- Instant Messaging: A tool such as Gmail/Gtalk that lets you create virtual networks of your partners, members, allies, advisors, pathfinders, other customers and potential customers, and people in your community, and then send and receive archivable instant messages (IM "chat threads"), electronic files, Web links, e-mails, and voice-to-voice calls by free Voice-over-Internet-Protocol [VoIP]). This is how much of Generation Millennium communicates—they've declared e-mail dead and are only willing to invest time and energy in real-time communication technologies.
- Desktop Videoconferencing: There are a variety of free or nearly free tools that allow you to conduct virtual meetings with almost exactly the same "presence" that you can receive face-to-face. They generally feature VoIP for audio, ability to broadcast the speaker's face by Webcam, the ability to "show" presentations and documents in real time to all participants, as you talk about them ("screen-sharing"), and change them on the fly as a result of the discussion, an archive that all participants can use to upload and download files or recordings of your virtual

meetings, and a list of all participants online with the capacity to send private IM "chat" between participants or publicly to all participants.

- Blogs: These should be used sparingly, since the technology is still not very user-friendly and they can be time-consuming. Blogs ("diaries" of articles that you can post anytime, categorize by subject, open or restrict access to, and "publish" or "subscribe to" easily using a transmission technology called RSS) are best suited to specialized newsletters (you might use them to manage the continuous environmental scan you use for your research), managing and routing information among diverse and remote communities of practice or communities of interest, and capturing the knowledge of "subject matter experts."

- Virtual Reality: There are some new tools, such as Second Life, that hold tremendous promise for meetings, Open Space problem-solving and brainstorming events (Open Space methodology was described in Chapter 3), and training events, when the participants just can't get together physically. But beware: Although this kind of "virtual presence" technology is likely to become ubiquitous in the next generation, it's still early days. Only experiment with this if you have lots of time, and a patient and technology-savvy group to work with.

The resource guide at the end of this book has more information about social-networking applications.

There is a lot of dubious "conventional wisdom" out there about networking. About the need to be aggressive. About the importance of exchanging business cards. About only networking with "key decision-makers." About the art of small talk. About exaggerated politeness. About being everything but yourself.

It is important to do your research before networking events. Learn who specifically you need or want to meet. Find out as much as you can about them, and where you are likely to meet them, or where you are likely to meet someone who can introduce you to them. And don't limit yourself to "secondary" (Internet and library) research. Talk to existing contacts to unearth information about your target contacts that no one else has (but be careful to verify it). Many networking "events" that are organized for you are a waste of time—you'll meet mostly other people looking to meet people who aren't there. Usually, the best networking events are those you have deliberately managed to get yourself invited to.

A great way to make a good first impression at networking events is to develop "elevator speeches." First impressions are important, and a brief, clear, compelling, rehearsed (but natural-sounding) twenty-to-thirty-second statement, prepared for and delivered to a specific target contact when you first meet, can be powerful. They shouldn't be the first thing you say, of course, but you shouldn't wait too long. They should be unique (something only you could or would say), personal and engaging, but not fawning, all about the other person, not about you, and should suggest how you might be able to help the other person. Hard work, but worth it.

> A great way to make a good first impression is to develop "elevator speeches."

You never know which members of your networks will turn out to be the most important, so don't underestimate the strength of "weak ties." Many of the critical successes in your personal and professional life will come through someone who knows the person who will ultimately enable that success (future customer, employer, best friend, or spouse), *not* through a direct, planned, or serendipitous contact with that person him- or herself. Those "friend of a friend," two- and three-degrees-of-separation contacts need to be nurtured and they need to be sincere—if you're just using someone to get to someone else, they'll know, and the outcome won't be pretty. But there can be an implicit "exchange of favors" among weak ties—"if you introduce me to X, I'll introduce you to Y." Reciprocity is acceptable.

> Don't underestimate the strength of "weak ties." Many successes in your life will come through someone who knows the person who will ultimately enable that success, not through a direct contact with that person him- or herself.

Women are often better networkers than men because, in my experience, women generally *listen better* and know that asking another person questions is a great way to engage them and draw them out. The objective of asking questions is to learn how you can help the other person, not to set him or her up for your sales pitch. Networking is not about selling (your product or yourself), and if you try to sell too hard or too early, you not only will fail but also won't get a second chance. If you understand the other person's needs, and can gently suggest that you might be able to help him or her meet those needs, you've succeeded.

An important rule in dealing with people in your networks is: Never lie, and don't tolerate deception from others in your network. Even being associated with dishonest people can seriously hurt your networking efforts, and if you yourself get a reputation for dishonesty or exaggeration, you're toast. Always be genuine—people have great bullshit detectors. A classic example of this kind of well-intentioned but disastrous deceit is the guy who calls you up and asks to "interview" you, when his real motivation is to land a job or contract with your company, using you as his research tool.

Learning to be a good conversationalist is essential to effective networking. Understand that every conversation is an implicit contract. The person who you're talking to has an objective in talking to you (which might be as simple as extracting him- or herself from the conversation ASAP). You have an objective in talking to that person. Those objectives may not be clear at the moment of first conversation, but one way or another they'll crystallize quickly. Like a dance, one person needs to lead. (Both people trying to lead is not uncommon, but pretty ungraceful.) The lead may switch back and forth, and that's all part of the implicit contract that guides and steers the conversation. That's why listening is so important, reading the body language, establishing trust and rapport. Until you both understand the implicit contract, there can be no real conversation, and without real conversation, there can be no real relationship. This is very subtle, but very important stuff. The only way to be good at it is through lots of practice.

If you say you're going to do something in a conversation, that's a commitment. Do it, quickly. Otherwise, you'll have a reputation for breaking promises you'll never live down. Follow through and follow up, promptly. And if you do establish a good relationship, don't just walk away—ask for a follow-up meeting, or, if you've really impressed and you know it's now or never, don't hesitate to ask directly for what you want.

Storytelling is a key skill of good conversation, so learn and practice telling memorable stories effectively. Nothing is more engaging, or more subversively effective, and nothing cuts through the ice better than a well-told story. That's why the best speeches always start with them.

> Storytelling is a key skill of good conversation, so learn and practice telling memorable stories effectively.

It's also important to prune your networks. Although there's no hard-and-fast rule, many experts believe that it's impossible to maintain meaningful relationships with more than about 150 people at a time. It's like juggling—too many balls in the air spells disaster. Do triage: Some relationships will grow just fine with no attention. Others aren't going anywhere, no matter how hard you work at them. Focus on the third group—those that will blossom with investment, but not without. And large networks, unmanaged, can allow a few disreputable people to creep in unnoticed, whose presence in your networks will taint you by association.

Finally, you have to manage your networks constantly, as you would manage any investment of your business. Occasionally sit down and go through your network list and evaluate each relationship, what its value is to you, what needs to be done, and which ones are most important and most urgent. Don't let the urgent relationships

> Networks are an investment—like gardens, they need to be tended, weeded, watered, and at the right time, harvested.

consume all your time so there is no time left for the important ones. Networks are an investment-like gardens, they need to be tended, weeded, watered, and at the right time, harvested.

By contrast with networks, business *alliances* are more formal, fixed-term or indefinite-life contractual arrangements between two or more businesses to achieve shared objectives. They may help you to do any of the following:

Collaborate on major projects: Creating a proposal or project team to bid jointly or to make a pitch that requires more capability than your business alone can offer, or where the customer wants bundled products or services. In this sense, an alliance is a bit like a subcontracting arrangement, but with a more equal partnership.

Joint purchasing: Forming a buying group with competitors or others buying the same supplies, to increase purchasing power and lower costs.

R&D / new product development: Sharing the cost and risk of leading-edge research. Bringing more skills, ideas, piloting capability, and funding to the New Product Development process than any single company can garner.

Joint marketing: Marketing alliances can include competitors in an industry (as with multidealer auto showrooms), enterprises at different points in a supply chain (as when a wholesaler and retailer collaborate), or even enterprises in unrelated industries (such as house builders who promote a furniture company's products in their model homes).

Licensing: Innovative enterprises can recognize opportunities to license an idea from one industry and apply it to a completely different industry, with the developer and the licensor of the idea sharing the revenues from its application.

Leveraging skills: Entrepreneurs can ally with think tanks, educational institutions, or other organizations to obtain inexpensive knowledge, consulting advice, and skilled partners.

There are three critical success factors to a good business alliance: The first is communication. Because alliances are between enterprises that each have their own structures and communication protocols, there is a tendency for alliance partners to each focus on their role in the partnership and undercommunicate (and undercollaborate) with their alliance partners. This can result in misunderstandings, unmet or unreasonable expectations, and important tasks falling between the cracks.

The second is goal and role clarity. Each enterprise in the alliance needs to understand the others' goals (objectives for participating in the alliance) and roles to ensure that conflicts and gaps are minimized and expectations are met.

Finally, there is what I call measures and commitment. Each enterprise in the alliance needs to have some skin in the game, or its participation in alliance activities will be subordinated to its own internal activities and priorities. And there need to be agreed-upon, objective measures, targets, and deadlines so that each enterprise's performance can be assessed and, if necessary, improved.

The value that your Natural Enterprise gets out of networking and alliances will be a function of three things: The up-front work you spend in preparing for, researching, and planning for network and alliance activities; the amount of quality time you invest in the networking and alliance activities themselves; and the depth of your communication skills.

An essential element of business relationships, especially in Natural Enterprises, is *reciprocity*. The *Oxford English Dictionary* describes reciprocity this way:

> This refers to exchanges between individuals or communities who are symmetrically placed, that is they are exchanging things more or less as equals: a sort of gift exchange. One gift does not have to be followed by another at once, but an obligation is created every time a gift is given and this needs to be reciprocated. Anthropologist Marshall Sahlins suggests that amongst close kin gifts are freely given with no expectation of return.

You can see that, because there is no expectation of return, reciprocity only flourishes in relationships of trust, and once again, this is an advantage of Natural Enterprises over traditional corporations. It embodies the idea of generosity; when this can be engendered in a relationship, it is very powerful and can sustain and simplify much of the work in any enterprise. In some Asian cultures, this idea of trust and reciprocity is the very embodiment of all business relationships.

One of the most interesting phenomena of the last decade has been the emergence of what has been called the Gift Economy. This is an entire undercurrent of economic activity based on the principle of reciprocity. Some examples include the creation of free software through open-source development; the peer-to-peer sharing of files among people who cannot afford to buy their own personal copies; the unrestricted and open sharing of information (some of it the results of lifelong work) among scientific peers to advance collective understanding; the philanthropy of many foundations, cooperatives, and "fraternal" organizations; and the new Internet-enabled concept of "peer production." In each case, people give their time, energy, and work products without expectation of return, and, when enough people do so, everyone benefits.

Good relationship building requires tact, rehearsal, practice, articulateness, brevity, clarity, excellent listening skills, and generosity. But it also can be fun, and in every sense one of the most rewarding aspects of Natural Enterprise.

The power of community

Natural Enterprises have one final advantage in difficult times over large, inflexible corporations—*community.*

In a crisis, we turn to those we love and trust for help and to offer help. Natural Enterprises cultivate this sense of deep community at two levels—internally among their partners, and externally with those in their customers, networks, alliances, and the physical neighborhoods where they earn a living. These can be a source of enormous strength in times when sacrifice and struggle may be needed.

Diana Leafe Christian has written a book called *Creating a Life Together*,[1] about establishing what are called "intentional communities" where people who are tired of anonymous, unfriendly neighborhoods can choose to live together with common purpose, respect, and love (like the communes of the 1960s).

In this book, she outlines the process of *creating community*. This process precisely parallels the process for creating Natural Enterprises outlined in this book: deciding on your Purpose, finding members, agreeing on vision and operating principles and terms of membership, deciding what the community will do, managing community relationships, and making the community resilient and sustainable.

In a real sense, a Natural Enterprise is a community within a community, and the principles and processes and values of the Natural Enterprise community and the neighborhood community in which it operates reflect and reinforce each other.

In his book *The Company We Keep*[2], John Abrams explains how the dynamics of his company and the dynamics of the greater community in which it is located interact powerfully, and how his company and his community partner and help build and strengthen each other. It is essential that a Natural Enterprise be involved and active and engaged in building and helping the neighborhood that is its home, and draw in return strength from that larger community.

I think one of the things that is so appealing about Natural Enterprise, beside the fact that it is instinctive and joyful, is that in our modern world we long for a renewed sense of community, to *belong* to a place as part of a group of people with common Purpose, and, as Dave Smith argues so eloquently[3], *To Be of Use*, of service, to that community. Natural Enterprise, as a community within a larger community, gives us that sense of belonging, Purpose, and usefulness twice over.

Some brilliant minds have recognized and understood the importance of community in all human endeavor:

> Human beings will be happier—not when they cure cancer
> or get to Mars or eliminate racial prejudice or flush Lake

Erie but when they find ways to inhabit [natural] communities again. That's my utopia.—Kurt Vonnegut

I am of the opinion that my life belongs to the community, and as long as I live it is my privilege to do for it whatever I can.—George Bernard Shaw

We are all longing to go home to some place we have never been—a place half-remembered and half-envisioned we can only catch glimpses of from time to time. Community. Somewhere, there are people to whom we can speak with passion without having the words catch in our throats. Somewhere a circle of hands will open to receive us, eyes will light up as we enter, voices will celebrate with us whenever we come into our own power. Community means strength that joins our strength to do the work that needs to be done. Arms to hold us when we falter. A circle of healing. A circle of friends. Someplace where we can be free.—Starhawk

Why people would rather do business with a Natural Enterprise

Traditional corporations rely on a few "competitive advantages" (aside from using their power to lobby governments for subsidies, tax breaks, trade agreements, and other favors and forming oligopolies to reduce choice and fix prices) to attract customers and try to dominate their markets.

These "competitive advantages" are: recognition, popular brand, low price, and efficiency. They come at a huge cost.

- The popular brand comes at a cost of reduced choice and variety.
- The low price comes with an horrific social and environmental price tag, which these corporations "externalize" to us as citi-

zens, taxpayers, unemployed and underemployed workers, and sufferers from the effects of environmental degradation.

- The efficiency comes at a cost of quality, service, attention, and care. These corporations reduce us from people to mere consumers, and they are driven to push us to buy more and more, of the same stuff everyone else buys, and reduce us to automatons who, in the words of one outspoken entrepreneur[4] become merely "gullets who live only to gulp products and crap cash."

Many people are beginning to rebel against the offerings of these large, faceless, global oligopoly corporations, and rediscover the advantage of buying local, carefully crafted products and services from producers who actually care about what they do and the people they do it for. This is what Natural Enterprise is all about.

> **Many people are beginning to rediscover the advantage of buying local, carefully crafted products and services from producers who actually care about what they do and the people they do it for.**

The advantages of dealing with a Natural Enterprise as customers and community members are:

- Personal relationship: knowledge, trust, partnership, friendship, even love,
- Customization: the ability to *really* have it your way,
- Local just-in-time service: responsibility, responsiveness,
- Superior innovation,
- No sales pressure: since the Natural Enterprise is not dependent on growth for survival, and already knows that the customer needs what they produce, and only needs to be shown how the Natural Enterprise's market meets that need,
- Reciprocity: since the Natural Enterprise is part of the community, and can "afford" to be generous,
- No corporatist costs to pass on: Natural Enterprises have no large management salaries, no big markups to achieve the high

return on investment demanded by shareholders, and no heavy advertising, marketing, transportation, or packaging costs,

- Resilience: because of their superior improvisational capacity and focus on customers' evolving needs and effectiveness rather than efficiency, Natural Enterprises are more resilient and sustainable, and won't leave town or go broke when economic or market conditions change,
- Quality and durability: no tainted crap from indifferent factories half a world away,
- Appeal to altruism: It feels good to do business with a Natural Enterprise that is good to its people, its community, and its environment and good for the local economy.

Give people a choice, and it's pretty obvious whom they'll choose to do business with. They're just waiting for you, and your Natural Enterprise, to give them that choice.

This brings us to the end of the journey to discover the natural work you were meant to do and how to do it. It is also the start of your personal journey to create *your* Natural Enterprise, to *realize* it, and bring it to life.

Are you ready? This book's final section, following the Chapter 6 case study will show you the first steps on that personal journey.

CHAPTER 6 CASE STUDY
The value of relationship with community

South Mountain

John Abrams's book *The Company We Keep* is the story of South Mountain Company, a Natural Enterprise with all of the qualities necessary to be sustainable, responsible, joyful. Those qualities include:

- It's egalitarian, not hierarchical.
- It adapts to circumstances and lets solutions to problems emerge, rather than "imposing" prescribed solutions.
- It's collaborative, not competitive.
- It buys respectfully, and finances purchases organically, rather than by beating suppliers down to the lowest price and then depending on low interest rates and government subsidies and "incentives" to stay afloat.
- It communicates its products virally, not through advertising and marketing.
- It strives for responsibility, effectiveness, and zero waste, rather than externalizing its costs and wastes for short-term profit.
- It evolves through innovation rather than through growth.
- It identifies and satisfies needs, rather than trying to create them.
- Its strategies are improvisational, not preemptive.

Abrams's story is detailed and refreshingly candid—he admits to the bad decisions, false starts, missteps, and the continuing work in progress that his enterprise is. He gives us the unvarnished truth—what really works, and what doesn't. South Mountain, a homebuilding enterprise on Martha's Vineyard, is based on eight operating principles:

1. Workplace democracy: Every employee is an owner, and control of the enterprise is vested collectively in its thirty partners.
2. Sustainability without growth: "We think about 'enough' rather than 'more,'" he writes. South Mountain adopts Thomas Princen's principles of sufficiency,[5] and vows never to grow beyond what Malcolm Gladwell calls the "rule of 150" (the maximum number of people with whom anyone can sustain deep, healthy social relationships[6]).
3. Goals of well-being, not wealth: Profit is merely one means of achieving meaningful goals that benefit all the partners and the community in which they work.

4. Commitment to place and community: The island is a place South Mountain's people live in, know intimately, care about, and strive to make a better place for all.

5. Everyone doing what they do best: The idea of craftsmanship, of pride in excellence, of doing what its people do well and are passionate about, imbues everything the company does.

6. Conserving communities: Building community in an age of restlessness and forced transience is a great challenge. Conserving what matters—love, deep relationships, local economies, the natural environment and all its inextricably intertwined elements—depends on people being there, for a lifetime, who care, conserving the community.

7. Being an integral part of the community: This means taking an active part in community activities and investing time, energy, and resources in problem-solving that extends far beyond the immediate interests of the company.

8. Thinking long term: Abrams calls this "cathedral building," citing Charles Handy. It is all about imagining inspiring possibilities and then working toward their realization, with the knowledge that this will benefit future generations, not today's, and that that is a good thing.

Abrams writes: "If we are lucky in life, work becomes an expression of who we are and one of our most important anchors of meaning."

• •

ONCE YOU'VE FINISHED THE BOOK
next steps

Now you understand the journey from wage slavery, chronic under-employment, dread about job prospects, and learned helplessness to Natural Enterprise and working naturally.

You already have begun the journey in the process of thinking about your Gift, your Passion, and your Purpose, and about unmet needs, possibilities, and innovations, in overcoming your fears about entrepreneurship and learning about the process, capacities, and knowledge involved in natural work.

Discovering and then "realizing" what you (and your prospective Natural Enterprise partners) were meant to do takes some time, effort, and thought, but it is not a difficult, frightening, or risky process. It is quite natural, the process by which indigenous and nonhuman cultures instinctively make a living for themselves and those they love.

It begins with self-knowledge and the discovery of your Gift, your Passion, and your Purpose, and then discovery of your Community, the partners you were meant to make a living with. It continues with research to find important unmet needs that are "on Purpose," and imagining possibilities, innovating solutions, and then collaboratively and resiliently improvising and "realizing" those solutions—bringing them to fruition and making them real.

Working naturally is as simple as that.

There are three "next steps," now that you've finished the book:

First, check out the Web sites that were designed to accompany the book, and to help you make your Natural Enterprise a reality:

Finding Natural Partners http://NaturalEnterprises.org/partners/—This is a social-networking tool that allows you to write about your Gift, your Passion, and your Purpose, and find partners with complementary abilities and shared values and life goals.

The Natural Enterprise Community http://NaturalEnterprises.org/community/—This is a venue for sharing your success (on your own terms) stories, war stories, challenges, and advice with other Natural Entrepreneurs. "Experts" may chime in, but experience suggests the most valuable advice comes freely from those who have faced similar issues themselves in their own enterprises.

The Natural Collaboratory http://NaturalEnterprises.org/collaboratory/—This is an idea market with a difference—the only investments in this "market" are your time, energy, and enthusiasm. No money changes hands and no "selling" is permitted. This is a place to:

- Float ideas;
- Do some secondary research;
- Get the "crowd" of prospective customers and coworkers to tell you what they think; and,
- Work in Open Space and Peer Production to bring ideas to light and then to fruition.

Next, continue learning. Go out and talk with entrepreneurs in your community, especially those you meet through the Natural Entrepreneur Web sites above, and those who have a reputation for sustainability, responsibility, and really loving their work. You will learn much more from other entrepreneurs than from any book, and most entrepreneurs love to talk about their work and show others what has worked for them.

The endnotes that follow are organized by chapter, and include a resource guide of recommended books, articles, and Web sites where you can learn more about the subject of that chapter.

Finally, just begin. In an earlier chapter I explained the importance of intentionality. There is great power in intention, especially when what you intend is something that is completely natural and attainable by everyone with an investment of time, energy, and patience. Make a list of what you need to do to create *your* Natural Enterprise, and each week commit to making progress on one item on that list.

> Finally, *just begin.* There is great power in intention

Once you begin, the journey to Natural Entrepreneurship will take on a momentum of its own. If you picked this book up, you must have been unhappy with the way you're making a living now. You owe it to yourself, and those you love, to discover or create a Natural Enterprise that will let you, at last, do what you were meant to do, with the people you were meant to do it with.

I wish you joy and success on your journey, and thank you for helping make the world a better, more sustainable, responsible, and happy place, just by doing what comes naturally.

DAVE POLLARD

January 2008

RESOURCE GUIDE
endnotes and additional readings

▲ indicates essential reading for those aspiring to create a Natural Enterprise

Endnotes

Introduction:

1. Paul Craig Roberts, "Nuking the Economy." In *Counterpunch*, February 11/12, 2006. www.counterpunch.org/roberts02112006.html.
2. Janine Benyus, *Biomimicry: Innovation Inspired by Nature* (New York: Harper Perennial, 2002). Also see the related Web site, www.biomimicry.net.
3. Joel Bakan, *The Corporation: The Pathological Pursuit of Profit and Power* (New York: Simon & Schuster, 2004). Also see the related Web site, www.the corporation.com.
4. Charles Handy, *The Age of Paradox* (Boston: Harvard Business School Press, 1994).
5. Peter Jay, *The Wealth of Man* (New York: Perseus Books, 2000).

Chapter 1:

1. ▲ Po Bronson, *What Should I Do With My Life?* (New York: Random House, 2002). Also see the related Web site, www.pobronson.com/index_what_should_I_do_with_my_life.htm.
2. Neil Crofts, *Authentic Business* (London: Capstone Publishing, 2005); Charles Handy, *The Age of Paradox* (Boston: Harvard Business School Press, 1994); and Daniel Quinn, *Beyond Civilization* (New York: Three Rivers Press, 1999).
3. ▲ Dick Richards, *Is Your Genius at Work?: Four Key Questions to Ask Before Your Next Career Move* (Mountain View, Calif.: Davies-Black Publishing, 2005).
4. Malcolm Gladwell, "Big and Bad." In *The New Yorker*, January 12, 2004. www .gladwell.com/2004/2004_01_12_a_suv.html.
5. Neil Crofts, *Authentic Business* (London: Capstone Publishing, 2005).
6. Po Bronson, *What Should I Do With My Life?* (New York: Random House, 2002).
7. The author's blog, *How to Save the World*. http://blogs.salon.com/0002007/ stories/2006/07/05/aboutTheAuthor.html.
8. Dick Richards, *Is Your Genius at Work?: Four Key Questions to Ask Before Your Next Career Move* (Mountain View, Calif.: Davies-Black Publishing, 2005).

9. George Monbiot, *Heat: How to Stop the Planet from Burning* (Boston: South End Press, 2007).

10. http://howtosavetheworld.ca.

11. Paul Graham, "How to Do What You Love." www.paulgraham.com/love.html.

Chapter 2:

1. James Kunstler, *The Long Emergency: Surviving the Converging Catastrophes of the Twenty-First Century* (New York: Atlantic Monthly Press, 2005).

2. Jim Merkel, *Radical Simplicity: Small Footprints on a Finite Earth* (Gabriola Island, B.C.: New Society Publishers, 2003).

3. Chris Corrigan, Open Space Web site. www.chriscorrigan.com/wiki/pmwiki.php?n=Main.OpenSpaceTechnology.

4. The classic text on future state Visions is Peter Schwartz's *The Art of the Long View* (New York: Currency Doubleday, 1991), which uses a scenario-planning approach to visioning; an alternate approach using storytelling is described in my blog article "Scenario Planning vs. Collective Vision: Imagining What's Possible," http://blogs.salon.com/0002007/2006/12/07.html#a1719.

5. James Surowiecki, "Mixed Motives." In *The New Yorker*, November 8, 2004. www.newyorker.com/archive/2004/11/08/041108ta_talk_surowiecki.

6. Michael Herman, "Inviting Language for Invitations and Openings." www.chriscorrigan.com/wiki/pmwiki.php?n=Main.InvitingLanguageForInvitation.

7. ▲ Dave Smith, *To Be of Use: The Seven Seeds of Meaningful Work* (Novato, Calif.: New World Library, 2005). Also see the related Web site, http://organictobe.wordpress.com/dave-smith/.

8. Peter Block, Stewardship (San Francisco: Berret-Kohler, 1993, 1996).

Chapter 3:

1. Michael Dertouzos, "Four Pillars of Innovation." In *Technology Review*, November 1999. www.technologyreview.com/Infotech/11991/?a=f.

2. RSS is a method, an Internet protocol, for subscribing to and publishing online content in a standard format called XML. Most major newspapers and periodicals, and many blogs, make their content subscribable in XML format. Subscribers (like you and me) set up an RSS "aggregator" page, use it to subscribe to all the XML "feeds" we want, and can then read everything we are interested in, online, on a single page, like a personalized electronic newspaper.

3. Shoshana Zuboff, *The Support Economy: Why Corporations Are Failing Individuals and the Next Episode of Capitalism* (New York: Viking Penguin, 2002).

4. Peter Drucker, *Innovation and Entrepreneurship* (New York: Harper Collins, 1985).

5. Maslow's hierarchy of needs, dating back to the 1940s, lists physiological, safety, and affinity needs as foundational to human nature, with esteem and self-actualization needs as less fundamental, only addressed when the baser needs have been met.

6. Nicholas Imparato and Oren Harari, *Jumping the Curve: Innovation and Strategic Choice in an Age of Transition* (San Francisco: Jossey-Bass, 1994).

7. James Surowiecki, *The Wisdom of Crowds: Why the Many Are Smarter Than the Few and How Collective Wisdom Shapes Business, Economies, Societies and Nations* (New York: Doubleday, 2004).

8. Chris Corrigan, Open Space Web site. www.chriscorrigan.com/wiki/pmwiki. php?n=Main.OpenSpaceTechnology.

9. Michael Herman, "Inviting Language for Invitations and Openings." www .chriscorrigan.com/wiki/pmwiki.php?n=Main.InvitingLanguageForInvitation.

10. Barbara Minto: *The Minto Pyramid Principle: Logic in Writing, Thinking and Problem Solving* (London: Private Publisher, 1996). The book and courses are available through www.barbaraminto.com.

11. ▲ Chan Kim and Renee Mauborgne, *Blue Ocean Strategy: How to Create Uncontested Market Space and Make Competition Irrelevant* (Boston, Harvard Business School Publishing, 2005).

12. Kathy Sierra, "How to Come Up With Breakthrough Ideas." In *Creating Passionate Users* (blog), November 30, 2005. http://headrush.typepad .com/creating_passionate_users/2005/11/how_to_come_up_.html.

Chapter 4:

1. During his tenure as editor of *HBR*, Levitt was quite pragmatic about the importance of innovation, arguing it was "one part inspiration, two parts discipline." He clearly believed that innovation was a learnable process that needed rigor in its application. That's what this chapter is all about.

2. ▲ Janine Benyus, *Biomimicry: Innovation Inspired by Nature* (New York: Harper Perennial, 2002). Also see the related Web site, www.biomimicry.net.

3. This BBC program was written by historian James Burke and is available on DVD. There is a companion book of the same name (New York: Macmillan, 1978—rereleased New York: Simon & Schuster, 2007).

4. Bill Buxton, *Sketching User Experiences* (San Francisco: Morgan Kaufmann, 2007). Buxton explains how sketching (improvisational design) increases innovation in the design process.

5. ▲ Clayton Christensen and Michael Raynor, *The Innovator's Solution* (Boston: Harvard Business School Press, 2003) is the best of the trilogy, which also includes *The Innovator's Dilemma* (Boston: Harvard Business School Press, 1997, no coauthor) and *Seeing What's Next* (Boston: Harvard Business School Press, 2004, coauthored with Erik Roth and Scott Anthony).

Chapter 5:

1. Unpublished proceedings of a symposium on the Organization of the Future organized by Boyden Institute, Toronto, September 16, 2005.

2. Peter Schwartz, *The Art of the Long View* (New York: Currency Doubleday, 1991), is an excellent resource on scenario planning; also Michael Raynor, *The*

Strategy Paradox (New York: Doubleday, 2007), explains the challenges of over-committing to one or two scenarios or not committing to any.

3. John Marshall and Bob McHardy, *Principles of Self-Management* (New York, Selection Testing, 1999).

4. Jeffrey Rayport, "The Virus of Marketing." In *Fast Company*, December 1996. www.fastcompany.com/online/06/virus.html.

5. Malcolm Gladwell, *The Tipping Point: How Little Things Can Make a Big Difference* (New York: Little, Brown & Company, 2000). Also see the related Web site, www.gladwell.com/tippingpoint/index.html.

6. Information on the history and advantages of the cooperative form of organization in different countries are available on the Web site of the International Co-operative Alliance at www.ica.coop/al-ica/.

7. The Mondragon Cooperative's Web site is at www.mcc.es/ing/index.asp.

8. Neil Crofts, *Authentic Business* (London: Capstone Publishing, 2005).

Chapter 6:

1. Diana Leafe Christian, *Creating a Life Together: Practical Tools to Create Ecovillages and Intentional Communities* (Gabriola Island, B.C.: New Society Publishers, 2003).

2. ▲ John Abrams, *The Company We Keep: Reinventing Small Business for People, Community, and Place* (White River Junction, Vt.: Chelsea Green Publishing, 2005). Also see the related Web site, www.somoco.com.

3. ▲ Dave Smith, *To Be of Use: The Seven Seeds of Meaningful Work* (Novato, Calif.: New World Library, 2005). Also see the related Web site, http://organictobe .wordpress.com/dave-smith/.

4. Jerry Michalski, possibly the world's best networker, is CEO of Sociate; his Web site is at www.sociate.com.

5. Thomas Princen, The Logic of Sufficiency (Cambridge, MA: MIT Press, 2005).

6. Malcolm Gladwell, *The Tipping Point: How Little Things Can Make a Big Difference* (New York: Little, Brown & Company, 2000). Also see the related Web site, www.gladwell.com/tippingpoint/index.html.

Additional readings and resources

Chapter 3:

- On Intractable Problems: The CogNexus Institute's Web site on "wicked" problems is at http://www.cognexus.org/id42.html.
- On Discovering Needs in Your Own Community: Wayne Roberts and Susan Brandum, *Get a Life* (Toronto: Get a Life Publishing House, 1995, out of print). A summary of this book can be found on my blog at http://blogs.salon .com/0002007/2006/07/06.html.

- On Finding Unmet Needs by Paying Constant Attention: My blog article, "Observations --> Opportunities." http://blogs.salon.com/0002007 /2005/07/12.html.
- On Tapping the Wisdom of Crowds: My blog article http://blogs.salon .com/0002007/2004/11/15.html.

Chapter 4:

On Innovation in Business:

- Peter Drucker, *Innovation and Entrepreneurship* (New York: Harper Collins, 1985).
- Gary Hamel, *Leading the Revolution: How to Thrive in Turbulent Times by Making Innovation a Way of Life* (Boston: Harvard Business School Press, 2000).
- Tom Peters, *The Circle of Innovation: You Can't Shrink Your Way to Greatness* (New York: Vintage, 1999).
- Michael Porter, *Competitive Strategy* (New York: Free Press, 1980).
- Henry Chesbrough, "Sometimes Success Begins at Failure." In *HBR Working Knowledge*, December 1, 2003. http://hbswk.hbs.edu/item/3807.html.
- Michel Robert, *Product Innovation Strategy* (New York: McGraw-Hill, 1995).
- Michael Schrage, *Serious Play: How the World's Best Companies Simulate to Innovate* (Boston: Harvard Business School Press, 1999).
- Erik Von Hippel, *The Sources of Innovation* (New York, Oxford University Press, 1988, revised 1994).
- Chuck Frey's *Innovation Tools* Web site, www.innovationtools.com.
- Mitch Ditkoff's *Idea Champions* Web site, www.ideachampions.com.
- Tom Kelley with Jonathan Littman, "The 10 Faces of Innovation." In *Fast Company*, October, 2005. www.fastcompany.com/magazine/99/faces-of-innovation.html.

On Imagination and Letting Ideas Emerge:

- Peter Senge, Otto Scharmer, Joseph Jaworski, and Betty Sue Flowers, *Presence: An Exploration of Profound Change in People, Organizations, and Society* (New York: Currency, 2005).
- Edward de Bono, *Serious Creativity: Using the Power of Lateral Thinking to Create New Ideas* (New York: HarperBusiness, 1993).
- My blog article, "Twelve ways to think differently." http://blogs.salon.com /0002007/2005/05/18.html.
- My blog article, "How to imagine." http://blogs.salon.com/0002007 /2005/10/10.html.

On Narrative and Storytelling:

- Robert Fulford, *The Triumph of Narrative: Story Telling in the Age of Mass Culture* (Toronto: House of Anansi Press, 1999).

- Steve Denning, *The Springboard: How Story Telling Ignites Action in Knowledge-Era Organizations* (Woburn, Mass.: Butterworth-Heinemann, 2001). Also see the related Web site, www.stevedenning.com.
- Dave Snowden's articles and presentations on narrative and storytelling are on his *Cognitive Edge* Web site at www.cognitive-edge.com/articlesbydave snowden.php and www.cognitive-edge.com/presentations.php respectively.

On Brainstorming:
- Article series from Mindtools. www.mindtools.com/brainstm.html.

On the Art of Conversation:
- My blog article, "Ten Steps to Great Conversations." http://blogs.salon.com /0002007/2006/09/07.html.

Chapter 5:
On the Gift Economy:
- My blog article, "The Gift Economy," is on the rationale for people giving others something of value for nothing, and how even when there are no prices, promises or debts, reciprocity works. http://blogs.salon.com/0002007/2005 /04/17.html.
- My blog article, "The Virtuous Cycles of the Gift Economy," which focuses on the trade-off between time and money and the value of unpaid work. http://blogs.salon.com/0002007/2006/12/06.html.

On Socially and Environmentally Sustainable Economies:
- My blog article, "After the Crash: A Blueprint for a Community-Based Economy," is a review and synopsis of Richard Douthwaite's online book *The Growth Illusion*, explaining how local economies work better than globalized economies in economic downturns or resource scarcities, and the role Natural Enterprises can play in them. http://blogs.salon.com/0002007/2005/11/10 .html.
- My blog article, "Environmental and Social Economics: A Primer," is a brief explanation of sustainable economics, focused on the work of Herman Daly. http://blogs.salon.com/0002007/2003/03/06.html.
- My blog article, "Duties Beyond Borders: Towards a Society Built on Respect for All Life," is a review and synopsis of Peter Brown's book *The Commonwealth of Life* (in Europe, released as *Ethics, Economics and International Relations*) about community-based economics based on principles of planetary stewardship. http://blogs.salon.com/0002007/2005/02/04.html.

Chapter 6:

- Umair Haque, *Peer Production* Web site. www.bubblegeneration.com/2005/11/peer-production-peer-production.cfm.

On Collaboration:

- Karl-Erik Sveiby, *The Business Value of Collaboration: Collaborative Climate Index,* presentation, 2004. www.ebrc.info/kuvat/Sveiby.pdf.
- Jon Katzenback and Douglas K. Smith, *The Wisdom of Teams* (New York: HarperBusiness, 1994).

On Social-Networking Tools:

- My blog article, "Social Networking in Business," is a review of various tools. http://blogs.salon.com/0002007/2006/12/05.html.

On Community-Based Enterprises:

- Business Alliance for Local Living Enterprises (BALLE) is as close as exists today to an association of Natural Enterprises; its Web site is at www.livingeconomies.org.
- Michael H. Shuman, *The Small-Mart Revolution* (San Francisco: Berrett-Koehler, 2006).

Case study Web sites and references

Briarpatch:

- Dave Smith, *To Be of Use: The Seven Seeds of Meaningful Work* (Novato, Calif.: New World Library, 2005). Also see the related Web site, http://organictobe.wordpress.com/dave-smith/.
- Peter Block, *Stewardship: Choosing Service Over Self-Interest* (San Francisco: Berrett-Koehler, 1993).

South Mountain:

- John Abrams, *The Company We Keep: Reinventing Small Business for People, Community, and Place* (White River Junction, Vt.: Chelsea Green Publishing, 2005). Also see South Mountain Company's Web site, www.somoco.com.
- Thomas Princen, *The Logic of Sufficiency* (Cambridge, Mass.: MIT Press, 2005). The principle of sufficiency is: Through collective, networked community-based self-management, allow an understanding of what would optimize the well-being of all life in the ecosystem, balancing all interests and appreciating natural constraints, to decide what is needed; agree to produce only, but

generously, what is needed, accepting and addressing all costs of production; collectively distribute what is needed to those who need it.

- Robin Dunbar, British anthropologist, proposed 150 as the "cognitive limit to the number of individuals with whom any one person can maintain stable relationships"; Malcolm Gladwell explains how this works in modern social and business relationships in *The Tipping Point* (New York: Little, Brown & Company, 2000).

Good Energy:

- Neil Crofts, *Authentic Business* (London: Capstone Publishing, 2005). The Good Energy Web site is at www.good-energy.co.uk.

Tall Grass Prairie Bread:

- This information is based on a report on CBC Radio's *The Vinyl Café*, June 10–11, 2007. The company Web site is at www.tallgrassbakery.ca.

WL Gore:

- WL Gore & Associates Web site is at http://www.gore.com/en_xx/.
- Alan Deutchman, "The Fabric of Creativity." In *Fast Company*, December 2004. www.fastcompany.com/magazine/89/open_gore.html.
- National Geographic, *The Green Guide: Teflon*. www.thegreenguide.com/teflon/.

Mountain Equipment:

- MEC's Web site is at www.mec.ca.

Interface Carpets:

- Interface's sustainability report and Interface Sustainability Model diagrams are at www.interfacesustainability.com/.
- Paul Hawken, Amory Lovins, and L. Hunter Lovins, *Natural Capitalism* (New York: Little, Brown & Company, 1999). The book can be downloaded free of charge at www.natcap.org.

Semco:

- Semco's Web site is at http://semco.locaweb.com.br/en/.
- Ricardo Semler, *Maverick* (New York: Warner, 1993). This is the founder's book about the company.

INDEX

E

earth, viii, xiii, 16
economic systems, vii, viii–ix, 4–6, 22–23, 159, 186
educational systems, 1, 11, 17, 18, 20, 34
egalitarianism, 24, 67, 81, 155, 177, 191
Einstein, Albert, 122
elevator speeches, 181
emotional intelligence. *See* instincts
employment. *See* work
energy, renewable, xiii, 64, 78, 169
energy crisis, 3, 64, 78, 159
entrepreneurship. *See* natural entrepreneurship
environmentalism, 15, 68
environmental scans, 92–94, 145, 159
experimenting, 135–137
ExxonMobil, 173–174

F

failure, 10, 13, 14–15
Fast Company magazine, 146, 163
fears, 10–18, 167, 193
finances, 10, 12, 14, 159, 160–163, 174–175
foods
    increase in price of, 159
    natural, xi–xii, 81–83, 120–121
freelancing, 1, 52, 57–58
fuel. *See* oil
Fuller, Buckminster, vii, 122

G

Gift Economy, 186
gifts
    defined, 31–32, 34–38
    examples of, 44–51
    and innovative solutions, 137
    and networking, 26
    and partnerships, 75–76
    and passions, 51–52
    of Pollard, 47–51, 57–59
    and shared purposes, 62–67
    and work charts, 47, 60, 61
Gladwell, Malcolm, 34, 163, 164, 191
global warming
    and industrialization, 22, 173–174
    and Morgana, 3, 63, 64
    and Pollard's purpose, 47, 49
Good Energy business, 169–170
Gore, Al, 49, 64
grocery stores, natural, xi–xii, 81–83, 120–121
Ground Zero, 157–158

H

Handy, Charles, 15–16, 192
happiness, 17, 97, 187–188
Harari, Oren, 106
Heat (Monbiot), 49
helplessness, 34, 193
hierarchies
    and case studies, 147, 191
    and corporations, 134, 155, 178
    and myths of entrepreneurship, 168
    and natural enterprises, 16, 67, 173, 177
hobbies, 54
humanity, 25
hunter-gatherer cultures, 17

I

ideas, 10, 12
imaginative skills, 18–19, 120–121, 122–128
Imparato, Nicholas, 106
improvisation, 157–159
independent consulting. *See* freelancing
industrialization, viii, 22–23, 36
infomediaries, 94
innovating solutions
    and case studies, 146–149
    and disruption, 12–13, 140–146
    guiding principles of, 128–130
    and imagining, 123–128
    introduced, 24, 25, 122–123
    landmines of, 138–140
    process of, 130–138
Innovation and Entrepreneurship (Drucker), 96–97
Innovator's Solution, The (Christensen and Raynor), 142, 143, 145
instincts, 18, 40, 102, 159
intentional communities. *See* communities
Interface Carpets, 147–149
internet
    and blogs, 49, 51, 71–72
    and new economy, 22
    and websites, viii–ix, 26–27, 60, 193–194
intersections, 24, 31–33, 51, 52, 55–56, 57, 59
investors, 12, 15
Is Your Genius at Work? (Richards), 31, 42–43

J

Janis, 3, 5, 64–67
Jean-Paul, 3, 5, 64–67
jobs. *See* natural entrepreneurship; work
Jumping the Curve (Harari and Imparato), 106